W9-BDX-491

Moments of Change

Parable

MOMENTS OF CHANGE

This edition has been printed exclusively for Parable®.

published by Multnomah Publishers, Inc.

International Standard Book Number: 1-59052-968-5

Printed in the United States of America

Edited by Anita K. Palmer

For information:
MULTNOMAH PUBLISHERS, INC.
601 N. LARCH ST.
SISTERS, OREGON 97759

06 07 08 09 10—10 9 8 7 6 5 4 3 2 1 0

MONDAY

THE PRAYER OF JABEZ

Jabez was more honorable than his brothers. His mother had named him Jabez, saying, "I gave birth to him in pain." Jabez cried out to the God of Israel, "Oh, that you would bless me and enlarge my territory! Let your hand be with me, and keep me from harm so that I will be free from pain." And God granted his request.

1 CHRONICLES 4:9–10

There's a principle in teaching called the principle of the irreducible minimum. That's when you boil everything down until it cannot be boiled down anymore. You have the essence, then, of whatever it is you're trying to teach.

One of those irreducible minimums of the Bible is tucked away in the middle of 1 Chronicles. There you'll find the prayer of Jabez. It touches on four major desires God has for everyone and boils them down to four simple requests that are repeated throughout the New Testament.

In fact, when you pray the prayer of Jabez, you're asking God to let you do everything He wants you to do.

—BRUCE WILKINSON, *Beyond Jabez*

Lord, bless me and enlarge my territory;
let Your hand be upon me, and keep me from harm.

TUESDAY

True Religion

What is more, I consider everything a loss compared to the surpassing greatness of knowing Christ Jesus my Lord, for whose sake I have lost all things. I consider them rubbish, that I may gain Christ and be found in him, not having a righteousness of my own that comes from the law, but that which is through faith in Christ—the righteousness that comes from God and is by faith.

Philippians 3:8–9

We all have difficulty, sometimes, in remembering the difference between experiencing a true relationship with the God of our salvation and experiencing merely the practice of religion.

We may do the spiritual things people expect us to do but never progress in the relationship. But Scripture, if we approach it honestly and let it be our guide, always presses us up against that relationship—the close, intimate walk with God that is so essential for true transformation. The deepest meaning of the Cross in its transforming power can only be understood experientially.

Don't ever equate knowing a doctrine with having experienced the reality of the truth.

—Henry Blackaby, *Experiencing the Cross*

Lord, help me to seek a deeper relationship with You today.

WEDNESDAY

Good News

I am not ashamed of the gospel, because it is the power of God for the salvation of everyone who believes: first for the Jew, then for the Gentile. For in the gospel a righteousness from God is revealed, a righteousness that is by faith from first to last, just as it is written: "The righteous will live by faith."

Romans 1:16–17

When it comes to fighting the desires of lust and other sins, the first impulse men and women have is to say, "Okay, I'm going to stop doing these bad things. I'm going to fix myself up. I'm going to get my life together."

But, sadly, so many of us can attest to the fact that we just can't do it. The sin of lust is another reminder of the reality that we need a Savior. That's the truth of the gospel—the Good News—which is this: that Jesus paid for my sins on the cross, that He obeyed God's law perfectly, and that by believing in Him, I'm not only forgiven, but I am clothed with His righteousness before God.

We can't save ourselves. We need a Savior.

—Joshua Harris, *Sex Is Not the Problem (Lust Is)*

Lord, thank You for paying for my sins; help me to rely on You, not myself.

THURSDAY

Letter to God: Eternal Treasures

Since, then, you have been raised with Christ, set your hearts on things above, where Christ is seated at the right hand of God.

Colossians 3:1

Dear God,

Help me set my eyes on the eternal treasures that You have stored up for me in heaven.

Deliver me from my senseless efforts to store up worldly things that won't last. You know how I struggle daily with wanting more, believing that I need more and working for more. But then I enter Your presence and realize that my true treasure is You.

I remember that Your truth says I came into this world with nothing and I'll leave with nothing. I remember Your promise about rewards You are waiting to give me when I enter Your kingdom, my eternal home. Give me a heart that longs to store up treasures in heaven.

Let me live for the day when we will see each other face-to-face. What a treasure that precious day will be.

Love,

Your princess, who treasures You

—Sheri Rose Shepherd, *Prayers to My King*

FRIDAY

Out of the Storm

Job 38:1–7

Then the Lord answered Job out of the storm. He said:
"Who is this that darkens my counsel
with words without knowledge?
Brace yourself like a man;
I will question you,
and you shall answer me.
Where were you when I laid the earth's foundation?
Tell me, if you understand.
Who marked off its dimensions? Surely you know!
Who stretched a measuring line across it?
On what were its footings set,
or who laid its cornerstone—
while the morning stars sang together
and all the angels shouted for joy?"

Lord, thank You for Your creation.

WEEKEND

UPHILL RACER

Be diligent in these matters; give yourself wholly to them, so that everyone may see your progress. Watch your life and doctrine closely. Persevere in them, because if you do, you will save both yourself and your hearers.

1 TIMOTHY 4:15–17

If you're on a bike ride and the entire ride is downhill, you'll get to the end of it. If it's a race, you might cross the finish line. Maybe you'll get a medal—but you won't have accomplished anything. A true race requires sweat and endurance and perseverance. That's what the Christian life is like as well.

A lot of us thought when we first became Christians that the Christian life would be an exciting adventure twenty-four hours a day. But some days you wake up and you feel down. You feel depressed. Like things aren't going your way and you wonder, *Why, what's going on with my life?* Those are the times when a Christian needs to persevere. We need to push through. We need to have our training kick in.

When you're down, when you're depressed, you've got to train. You've got to read your Bible. You've got to go to church. That way, when you get through it, you've truly accomplished something.

—RYAN DOBSON, *2 Live 4*

Lord, help me to push through the down times.

MONDAY

Beginning with the People of God

Repent, then, and turn to God, so that your sins may be wiped out, that times of refreshing may come from the Lord, and that he may send the Christ, who has been appointed for you—even Jesus.

Acts 3:19–20

In one year in America, more than 957,000 marriages end in divorce. More than 15,000 people are murdered. A million pregnancies are aborted. And more than 30,000 people take their own lives.

The healing of the land begins with the people of God. The nation changes when God's people change. The culture changes when the church changes. And that change begins when we repent.

America needs to change. And the change begins with me. You probably don't have any trouble with the first part of that thought. But are we willing to say the change begins with me?

The healing of the land begins with the people of God.

—Max Lucado, *Turn*

Lord, help me to pray for change, beginning with me.

TUESDAY

Table for All

Then Jesus said to his host, "Although they cannot repay you, you will be repaid at the resurrection of the righteous."

Luke 14:12–14

One Sabbath Jesus went to the house of a prominent Pharisee for a meal. He noticed that people were carefully choosing seats according to status. He said to the host, "The next time you give a dinner, don't ask your friends, your brothers, your relatives, or your rich neighbors, lest they invite you back and you be repaid—invited back for dinner. Instead," Jesus said, "when you give a feast, invite the poor, the maimed, the lame, the blind and you will be blessed, because they cannot repay you."

How will you be blessed? You'll have that warm, inner feeling, right? You've done it. I've done it. But that's exactly the opposite of what Jesus meant. Here's what He said. "You'll be blessed for you shall be repaid at the resurrection of the just." Do you realize that the blessing will take place after you're dead? What you do today matters forever.

—Bruce Wilkinson, *A Life God Rewards*

Lord, help me to show true hospitality to all and not be concerned about appearances.

WEDNESDAY

The True Vine

John 15:1–8

*"I am the true vine, and my Father is the gardener.
He cuts off every branch in me that bears no fruit, while every
branch that does bear fruit he prunes so that it will be even
more fruitful. You are already clean because of the word I have
spoken to you. Remain in me, and I will remain in you.
No branch can bear fruit by itself; it must remain in the vine.
Neither can you bear fruit unless you remain in me.*

*I am the vine; you are the branches. If a man remains in me and I in him,
he will bear much fruit; apart from me you can do nothing.
If anyone does not remain in me, he is like a branch that is thrown away
and withers; such branches are picked up, thrown into the fire and burned.
If you remain in me and my words remain in you, ask whatever you wish,
and it will be given you. This is to my Father's glory,
that you bear much fruit, showing yourselves to be my disciples."*

---

*Lord, thank You for allowing us to be connected to You
intimately, like branches on a vine.*

THURSDAY

Time to Check Priorities

When the earth and all its people quake,
it is I who hold its pillars firm.

Psalm 75:3

Do you have a minute? We all do, right? More than fourteen hundred of them every day. Still, sometimes it's hard to figure out where they all go. There's the normal stuff, like working, sleeping, and waiting at red lights. But a big chunk of our time is discretionary—things we get to choose. And if you're not careful, you can spend a lot of your minutes on things that aren't important.

A good place to start is to evaluate your priorities. Even if you haven't consciously made the decision, you do have priorities. They're usually defined by three areas: your anxieties, your activities, and your ambitions. Once you determine what the priorities in your life are, then you can decide if you're actually majoring on the minors or not.

Jesus reminded us in the Sermon on the Mount to seek first His Kingdom and His righteousness. Whatever you do, be sure you make the Kingdom your first priority.

—Stuart Briscoe, *Time Bandits*

Lord, help me to evaluate my priorities in light of Your kingdom.

FRIDAY

Rocket Speed

But do not forget this one thing, dear friends: With the Lord a day is like a thousand years, and a thousand years are like a day. The Lord is not slow in keeping his promise, as some understand slowness. He is patient with you, not wanting anyone to perish, but everyone to come to repentance. But the day of the Lord will come like a thief. The heavens will disappear with a roar; the elements will be destroyed by fire, and the earth and everything in it will be laid bare.

2 Peter 3:8–10

Patience and perseverance may not be popular in our society. We want to eat fast, learn fast, shop fast. We want swift service on our insurance claims, rocket speed on our computer processors, and rapid advances and pay increases at our jobs.

However, patience and perseverance are, indeed, counseled in the Bible. God says a thousand years are as a watch in the night for the Lord. He is in no hurry. Rest assured that He will bring to pass that which is right for you and for the society in which we live.

—Pat Robertson, *Six Steps to Spiritual Revival*

Lord, thank You for your patience. Help me to persevere.

WEEKEND

He Cares About the Details

Cast all your anxiety on him because he cares for you.

1 Peter 5:7

Is God concerned about the details of your life? Does He care about the little things? Sure, the Bible says He has compassion for His people, but isn't that sort of an arm's-length sort of compassion, like a multimillionaire might feel as he writes a check for a poor child living on the other side of the world?

No. God's compassion is the intimate, heartfelt compassion of a father. He's not so preoccupied with running the universe that your concerns, even the little ones, somehow escape His notice. So if your problems today are piling so high you feel ready to stumble under the weight of them, stop and take Peter's good advice to cast all your anxiety and cares upon God, because He cares for you.

—Joni Eareckson Tada, *31 Days to Intimacy with God*

Lord, help me to turn to You for the little things as well as the big.

MONDAY

More than Conquerors

No, in all these things we are more than conquerors through him who loved us. For I am convinced that neither death nor life, neither angels nor demons, neither the present nor the future, nor any powers, neither height nor depth, nor anything else in all creation, will be able to separate us from the love of God that is in Christ Jesus our Lord.

Romans 8:37–39

When God does something, He does it thoroughly, exceeding abundantly above and beyond all that we could ask or think.

The victory He won for us on the cross, over the forces of spiritual evil, is an overwhelming and everlasting victory. As a result, we're not just conquerors; we're more than conquerors.

No spiritual force can ever separate you from God's love and the cross of Christ. Never act as though it can. Live the victory He has won for you, and let the world see it being lived out in your life.

—Henry Blackaby, *Experiencing the Cross*

Lord, help me to live as the victorious child of God I am.

TUESDAY

In the Margins

Jesus answered them, "It is not the healthy who need a doctor, but the sick. I have not come to call the righteous, but sinners to repentance."

Luke 5:31–32

Our world, our culture, our society—all have margins, just like the page of this book.

Margins are places occupied by people who seldom figure in with what the mainline world esteems. In the margins are where I find people like me—people with brokenness or pain or sin. The margins are places where you want to go and hide and keep to yourself. Yet inside, your soul is screaming for someone to come and love you and know you.

The beautiful thing about Christ is that He does know you, and He knows what it's like to be in the margins. In fact, it's in those margins that Jesus shows up and calls us to Himself to reimagine the beauty of life through the lenses of His love.

—Rick McKinley, *Jesus in the Margins*

Lord, thank You for ministering in the margins.

WEDNESDAY

The Lie of No Consequences

So the Lord God banished him from the Garden of Eden to work the ground from which he had been taken. After he drove the man out, he placed on the east side of the Garden of Eden cherubim and a flaming sword flashing back and forth to guard the way to the tree of life.

Genesis 3:23–24

One of the major lies of the devil is that sin carries no consequences.

When Adam and Eve sinned and were removed from the Garden of Eden, one consequence was that God was no longer close and accessible. Unfortunately, many people who are physically alive are spiritually dead. God is a long way away. Why? Because, like Adam and Eve, we believed the lie, acted on the lie, and now we're getting the repercussions of the lie.

Here's the truth: You can control the sin, but you cannot control the consequences. Clearly, then, it's better not to commit the sin so you don't have to wonder how far these consequences will extend.

—Tony Evans, *God Can Not Be Trusted*

Lord, help me to accept the consequences of my sin.

THURSDAY

The Right Key

"Here I am! I stand at the door and knock. If anyone hears my voice and opens the door, I will come in and eat with him, and he with me."

Revelation 3:20

I was in Atlanta to speak at the NBA All Stars chapel. When I checked in at the hotel, they gave me two keys, one for my room and for the concierge desk, because my room wasn't cleaned yet. I put them into my pocket and took the elevator to the concierge's room.

When I put the key in to open the door, it didn't open it. I slid it faster and then slower, then turned it over and around. No matter what I did, it wouldn't open the lock. Then I remembered there was another key in my pocket.

Could it be that you have two keys to life, what you believe and how you behave? They open different locks. And no matter how hard you try if you have the wrong key in your hand, it will not open the lock.

—Bruce Wilkinson, *A Life God Rewards*

Lord, You are the key to life. Help me to behave the way I say I believe—with You on the throne of my heart.

FRIDAY

The Art of Motorcycle Maintenance

Do not let this Book of the Law depart from your mouth; meditate on it day and night, so that you may be careful to do everything written in it. Then you will be prosperous and successful.

Joshua 1:8

I have a motorcycle, a 1979 Triumph Bonneville. Being that it's thirty years old, you've really got to watch it. It takes constant maintenance and care.

So when I'm riding it, I'm listening. I'm thinking, *Is that a rattle I've always had, or is it a new rattle?* A lot of times it runs perfectly, but every now and then I hear something that needs a little bit of work.

In my Christian walk it's the same thing. Most of the time things are going great. I'm doing well. My relationships are healthy. But every now and then there's a rattle, and I'm not quite sure what it is. To get back on the road it takes going back to the Owner's Manual of Life—that's the Bible.

—Ryan Dobson, *2 Live 4*

Lord, help me to be sensitive to my walk with You.

WEEKEND

Who Can Be Against Us?

Romans 8:31–39

What, then, shall we say in response to this? If God is for us, who can be against us? He who did not spare his own Son, but gave him up for us all—how will he not also, along with him, graciously give us all things? Who will bring any charge against those whom God has chosen? It is God who justifies. Who is he that condemns? Christ Jesus, who died—more than that, who was raised to life—is at the right hand of God and is also interceding for us. Who shall separate us from the love of Christ? Shall trouble or hardship or persecution or famine or nakedness or danger or sword? As it is written:

"For your sake we face death all day long;
we are considered as sheep to be slaughtered."

No, in all these things we are more than conquerors through him who loved us. For I am convinced that neither death nor life, neither angels nor demons, neither the present nor the future, nor any powers, neither height nor depth, nor anything else in all creation, will be able to separate us from the love of God that is in Christ Jesus our Lord.

Lord, thank You for being for us.

MONDAY

Learning to Live Grace

Do not merely listen to the word, and so deceive yourselves. Do what it says. Anyone who listens to the word but does not do what it says is like a man who looks at his face in a mirror and, after looking at himself, goes away and immediately forgets what he looks like. But the man who looks intently into the perfect law that gives freedom, and continues to do this, not forgetting what he has heard, but doing it—he will be blessed in what he does.

JAMES 1:22–25

We learn to live grace over a period of time. It doesn't come naturally for us. But the more we become like Jesus, the more natural it is for the character of Christ to be manifested in our thoughts and our lives.

The same thing is true with living out truth. Sometimes we look at truth and we say, "Boy, that's hard. I can't really grasp it." But the more we wrestle with God's truth, the more we study His Word, the more equipped we are to speak God's truth to those who need to hear it.

—RANDY ALCORN, *The Grace and Truth Paradox*

Lord, help me to wrestle with Your truth and live in grace.

TUESDAY

What Sin?

Once you were alienated from God and were enemies in your minds because of your evil behavior. But now he has reconciled you by Christ's physical body through death to present you holy in his sight, without blemish and free from accusation—if you continue in your faith, established and firm, not moved from the hope held out in the gospel. This is the gospel that you heard and that has been proclaimed to every creature under heaven, and of which I, Paul, have become a servant.

Colossians 1:21–23

I've seen this happen a dozen times. Someone really blows it. He falls into sin. The sin is upon his conscience, and he thinks to himself, *God is so mad at me. I can't confess the same sin again.*

Well, as far as God is concerned, if we have confessed a sin, He says, *What sin?* The Bible says He remembers our sins no more!

No matter how often you have blown it, no matter how often you have sinned, always time and time again keep returning to the Father in humble confession. Don't ever allow your sin to drive you away from Him. Return to Him where you belong.

—Erwin Lutzer, *After You've Blown It*

Lord, thank You for the reassurance of forgiveness.

WEDNESDAY

Strong Spiritual Roots

They will be called oaks of righteousness,
a planting of the Lord for the display of his splendor.

Isaiah 61:3

If someone were to ask you, "How do I develop strong spiritual roots for my family?" what would you say to them?

Our family became unshakable when we began to sink roots into the person of Jesus Christ. Those who are obedient to God, those who follow Jesus Christ, can become oaks of righteousness. If you want your family to be strong, if you want your relationships or your marriage to establish spiritual roots, then grow together in prayer, Bible study, worship, giving in service and sacrifice, fellowship, and sharing your faith with others.

By doing so, you'll find that you will become an oak of righteousness and your relationships will become unshakable.

—Dennis and Barbara Rainey, *Growing a Spiritually Strong Family*

Lord, help me to put down deep family roots.

THURSDAY

Letter to God: The Price

Set your minds on things above, not on earthly things.
For you died, and your life is now hidden with Christ in God.

Colossians 3:2–3

Dear God,

It's so amazing to me that You paid the price for my sin with Your life. You loved me before I ever even thought about You, yet too often I walk away from Your love.

Forgive me for taking Your presence and Your love for granted. Help me to value my life as the precious gift it is. I don't want to sell out to the world that's trying to steal my integrity, corrupt my character, and weaken my love for You.

Please protect me, guide me, and help me to spend my time here wisely. Show me how You want me to invest the talents and gifts You have given me for Your eternal purposes, and let me never forget the true and lasting value of what You did for me on the cross, the price You paid just for me.

Love,

Your princess, who is grateful for everlasting life

—Sheri Rose Shepherd, *Prayers to My King*

FRIDAY

One Step at a Time

You, my brothers, were called to be free. But do not use your freedom to indulge the sinful nature; rather, serve one another in love. The entire law is summed up in a single command: "Love your neighbor as yourself."

Galatians 5:13–14

It's tempting to be overwhelmed and even paralyzed as you discover the presence of lust in your life. There are so many temptations. You may think, *There are so many little battles that I have to face. Where do I possibly begin?*

I encourage people to just take one thing at a time. It might be the television you watch. It might be saying to yourself, "I'm not going to watch these shows." It might be a decision to guard your eyes more carefully at a certain time of day. Whatever it looks like for you—whatever the little battle is for you—pick one thing. Take small steps in that area. Ask for God's help.

And as you grow in that one place, you're going to see a strength in your own heart to resist lust in every area.

—Joshua Harris, *Sex Is Not the Problem (Lust Is)*

Lord, help me to talk to You throughout the day about every step I need to take to be victorious over my sins.

WEEKEND

Our Daily Grace

If I speak in the tongues of men and of angels, but have not love, I am only a resounding gong or a clanging cymbal. If I have the gift of prophecy and can fathom all mysteries and all knowledge, and if I have a faith that can move mountains, but have not love, I am nothing.

1 Corinthians 13:1–2

Christians sing about amazing grace. We talk about how by grace we are saved. And oftentimes, we somehow act as if all we really needed of God's grace was at that moment when we became a Christian. We forget that we need grace every day.

Every day we sin against almighty God. Every day we fall short. Every day we break our commitments to Him. We require grace from God every day.

But then, when we turn toward other people, we become hard and harsh in our expectations of their behavior. It's as if we can explain away all of our sinful behavior on the one hand, and then turn and expect nothing but perfect responses from those that we relate to every day.

—Richard Blackaby, *Putting a Face on Grace*

Lord, help me not to be all words and no action when it comes to love.

MONDAY

Face-to-Face

The priests and the captain of the temple guard and the Sadducees...were greatly disturbed because the apostles were teaching the people and proclaiming in Jesus the resurrection of the dead. They seized Peter and John, and because it was evening, they put them in jail until the next day. But many who heard the message believed, and the number of men grew to about five thousand.

Acts 4:1–4

We pulled in to a fast-food restaurant. There was an old man right out front who looked like he hadn't eaten for weeks. On the way inside, our younger daughter, Jennifer, said, "Dad, we should buy him a hamburger and some fries and a shake."

So we did. And as we drove away, our daughter said, "That was wonderful. I feel so good inside."

And I said, "That's great, sweetheart. But guess what Jesus said is coming. He said if you take care of meeting the needs of people who can't meet their needs themselves, you're going to be blessed, but you're going to be blessed at the resurrection of the just. Jesus linked what you do today with what is going to happen when you see Him face-to-face."

—Bruce Wilkinson, *A Life God Rewards*

Lord, help me to recognize heavenly actions in the everyday.

TUESDAY

Indescribable

The heavens declare the glory of God;
the skies proclaim the work of his hands.
Day after day they pour forth speech;
night after night they display knowledge.
There is no speech or language
where their voice is not heard.

Psalm 19:1–3

It can be quite intimidating to think of God as holy, as separate. As if we can never approach Him.

It's true that there really are no words to describe God. He is so other than us. He's so much bigger than us. In one of our songs, *Indescribable*, the very last line says, "Yet You know the depths of my heart and You love me the same."

What an amazing thought. That this holy God wants to draw close to you when you draw close to Him.

—Chris Tomlin, *The Way I Was Made*

Lord, thank You that You love even me.

WEDNESDAY

In Whose Image?

"You shall not make for yourself an idol in the form of anything in heaven above or on the earth beneath or in the waters below. You shall not bow down to them or worship them; for I, the Lord your God, am a jealous God."

Exodus 20:4–5

God knows that the thing we worship is what's going to take up most of our time. It's what we're going to become like. That's why God says to be careful pursuing the images of this world.

And ultimately, when you pursue the image of the world, you'll discover that it's like a man being married to a woman but having the picture of another woman in his wallet. It's like God saying, "You say you put Me first but you're seeking another." In the end, the Lord says, "Please put Me first. Nothing could thrill Me more and bless you more."

—Ron Mehl, *Right with God*

Lord, help me to put You first and seek no other lord of my life.

THURSDAY

A New Creation

"Behold, I will create
new heavens and a new earth.
The former things will not be remembered,
nor will they come to mind....
I will rejoice over Jerusalem
and take delight in my people;
the sound of weeping and of crying
will be heard in it no more."

Isaiah 65:17, 19

One day I had a remarkable time of meditation. I was thinking about the enormous responsibility that the Lord had taken on in creation. How much suffering was going on in the world. How many terrible things. I asked God, "Why did You do it?"

And the Lord spoke back to my spirit that He had created a new heaven and a new earth. His reward was to see that new heaven and new earth filled with men and women, boys and girls, who would be created in the knowledge and the image of Jesus Christ, His Son, for all eternity.

—Pat Robertson, *Six Steps to Spiritual Revival*

Lord, thank You for promising us a new heaven and a new earth.

FRIDAY

Stretched and Strong

We ought always to thank God for you, brothers, and rightly so, because your faith is growing more and more, and the love every one of you has for each other is increasing. Therefore, among God's churches we boast about your perseverance and faith in all the persecutions and trials you are enduring.

2 Thessalonians 1:3–4

Sometimes in life we feel persecuted. We feel like we're not being protected by God and we want to ask, "God, why aren't You protecting me? Can't You do a better job of this? And if You can, why don't You?" Look at David, a man after God, someone whom God truly loved. You can find some stark psalms of David, in which he cries out, "Lord, where are You? Why are my enemies winning? Why are they laughing at me?"

However, David's experiences stretched him. We can look at all the heroes of the Bible, and at each of our lives, and ask, *Is that what's going on? Am I being stretched? Am I growing?* Then we stop asking why? and start asking what? *What can I learn from this? What is God trying to show me? How can I grow as a Christian?* That will make us mature Christians. It almost makes us say, *let me* be persecuted. It's an honor to have to grow and be stretched in those situations.

—Ryan Dobson, *2 Live 4*

Lord, help me to accept Your stretching so I can be strong for You.

WEEKEND

Letter to God: Holy Wardrobe

Jesus called the Twelve and said, "If anyone wants to be first, he must be the very last, and the servant of all."

Mark 9:35

Dear God,

My heart feels burdened when I look at wardrobes of this world and how women will do anything to get attention and feel valued. Yet I confess that I am guilty of wearing some of them myself. Please help me stop conforming to this world. I don't want to be defined by a fashion designer any longer.

Lord, convict me of the clothes in my closet that make me look like someone other than Your princess. Set me free from being a slave to the world's fashions. Clothe me, instead, with the attributes of my Savior. Then use me to set the trends of holiness and purity.

From now on, may whatever I wear reflect my commitment to You. Use my identity in You to touch the hearts of people all around me. I'm ready to be Your model of life to the world.

Love,

Your princess, who wants to dress for You

—Sheri Rose Shepherd, *Prayers to My King*

MONDAY

Just Listen

Isaiah 1:2–3

Hear, O heavens! Listen, O earth!
For the Lord has spoken:
"I reared children and brought them up,
but they have rebelled against me.

The ox knows his master,
the donkey his owner's manger,
but Israel does not know,
my people do not understand."

Lord, please help me to listen to You more closely!

TUESDAY

By Streams of Water

Psalm 1

Blessed is the man
who does not walk in the counsel of the wicked
or stand in the way of sinners
or sit in the seat of mockers.
But his delight is in the law of the Lord,
and on his law he meditates day and night.
He is like a tree planted by streams of water,
which yields its fruit in season
and whose leaf does not wither.
Whatever he does prospers.
Not so the wicked!
They are like chaff
that the wind blows away.
Therefore the wicked will not stand in the judgment,
nor sinners in the assembly of the righteous.
For the Lord *watches over the way of the righteous,*
but the way of the wicked will perish.

Lord, thank You for Your streams of water.

WEDNESDAY

The Positive Energy of Negative Emotion

Be merciful to me, Lord, for I am faint;
O Lord, heal me, for my bones are in agony.
My soul is in anguish. How long, O Lord, how long?
Turn, O Lord, and deliver me; save me because of your unfailing love.

Psalm 6:2–4

God, please, please help me. I just don't know if I can go on."

Steve: Emotions can paralyze you. They can make you feel like things are hopeless. But the challenge is how do you take these emotions and turn them into something positive, something that makes you a stronger, a deeper, a better person?

Pam: One of the problems most of us have is that we've been taught that negative feelings are bad. But the grief we experience on the back side of a wound is a driving force. And that emotional energy is what presses us to examine ourselves, to examine our worldview, our beliefs in God. It's eventually what drives us to adjust to our loss. It's what energizes us to change.

—Dr. Steve Stephens & Pam Vredevelt, *The Wounded Woman*

Lord, help me to give You my emotions
and be open to growth.

THURSDAY

The Second Judgment

For this very reason, Christ died and returned to life so that he might be the Lord of both the dead and the living. You, then, why do you judge your brother? Or why do you look down on your brother? For we will all stand before God's judgment seat. It is written: "'As surely as I live,' says the Lord, 'every knee will bow before me; every tongue will confess to God.'" So then, each of us will give an account of himself to God.

ROMANS 14:9–12

When you accept Jesus Christ as your personal Savior, God forgives your sins. You're not going to be judged for your sins because you're given a gift. The gift is His forgiveness of your sins and eternal life.

But did you know that there's a second time of judgment coming? This judgment takes place after you are already in heaven. God has been writing in a book everything you've said and everything you've done.

You have time from right now until the moment you breathe your last breath to have whatever you want written in that book. And God is going to reward you on the basis of what you've done.

—BRUCE WILKINSON, *A Life God Rewards*

Lord, help me to realize how important it is to act out my faith in the real world.

FRIDAY

Willing to Engage

He died for us so that, whether we are awake or asleep, we may live together with him. Therefore encourage one another and build each other up, just as in fact you are doing.

1 Thessalonians 5:10–11

In 2003, college students Mike Yankoski and Sam Purvis spent more than five months living on the streets of America to learn what it means to be homeless.

A Nebraska-based youth group came to volunteer for a week at the Denver Rescue Mission. Watching the students engage in conversations with the men in the rehabilitation program was incredible. Because of their willingness to engage the men and find out what had led them to that rehabilitation point and what they wanted to do when they graduated—because they were willing to engage them, the men in the program were so encouraged.

You see, it's not just writing a check, although that's good. To be present at a ministry, that's when God really starts to move and work.

—Mike Yankoski, *Under the Overpass*

Lord, help me to be willing to be used by You in ministry.

WEEKEND

Unfathomable Greatness

I will exalt you, my God the King;
I will praise your name for ever and ever.
Every day I will praise you
and extol your name for ever and ever.
Great is the Lord *and most worthy of praise;*
his greatness no one can fathom....
My mouth will speak in praise of the Lord.
Let every creature praise his holy name for ever and ever.

Psalm 145:1–3, 21

The writer of Psalm 145 makes a huge promise. Here's a guy who says worship has worked its way up his priority list.

His greatness no one can fathom. That's an amazing statement. Whatever little gods I have in my life, whatever little idols I have in my life—their greatness can be fathomed. But God's greatness—nobody can fathom it. No one can find the bottom of His greatness.

Worship is for the glory of God, and He's a worthy God, this Creator who made the heavens and the earth. Worship matters.

—Louie Giglio, *The Air I Breathe*

Lord, help me to keep worship of You
constantly at the top of my priority list.

MONDAY

Hanging on to His Promises

I do not consider myself yet to have taken hold of [perfection]. But one thing I do: Forgetting what is behind and straining toward what is ahead, I press on toward the goal to win the prize for which God has called me heavenward in Christ Jesus.

PHILIPPIANS 3:13–14

So often we settle in with our sinful nature and decide that we just can't help it. We think we're bound to function that way, because that's just how we are. And so we end up canceling the practical effect of God's promises.

Instead, learn to recognize everything God has done for you and take full advantage of it. Accept His complete provision, and ask Him to help you understand and appropriate what He has supplied.

Come to Him and say, "Oh, Father in heaven, I know Your promises. I know that You have made available everything I need to live a godly life. And yet I just don't fully grasp how to implement these blessings. But if You'll show me, I will respond."

—HENRY BLACKABY, *Experiencing the Cross*

Lord, help me to cling to Your promises.

TUESDAY

SATAN'S FIRST LIE

"He was a murderer from the beginning, not holding to the truth, for there is no truth in him. When he lies, he speaks his native language, for he is a liar and the father of lies."

JOHN 8:44

The polygraph detects when someone is lying by recording changes in the body, such as blood pressure, heart rate, and respiration. When it comes to Satan, the only reliable lie detector is the Word of God.

Satan does not want us to believe that God exists, not in any real way. Why? You can do your own thing when there is no God. But when there is someone to whom you are accountable, that has to change the way you live and think.

Since the heart of Satan's rebellion is to get us to live independently from God, Satan removes God from the equation and creates substitute gods, namely ourselves or other things we create.

Thus you need to use the Word of God to detect Satan's first lie, that God really doesn't exist.

—TONY EVANS, *God Can Not Be Trusted*

Lord, help me to constantly guard against the enemy's lies.

WEDNESDAY

UNIQUE TO US

So, if you think you are standing firm, be careful that you don't fall! No temptation has seized you except what is common to man. And God is faithful; he will not let you be tempted beyond what you can bear. But when you are tempted, he will also provide a way out so that you can stand up under it.

1 CORINTHIANS 10:12–13

One of the most important things we can understand about how lust trips us up is to realize that it has a "custom-tailored" plan for our life. It's going to look different for different people. It's going to come at us in a unique way.

So we need to ask the question: Where am I tempted? Where are the locations, the times of days, or the environments or settings that are particularly difficult for me? And then we need to create our own custom-tailored plan for fighting back.

The issue is obeying God, responding to the conviction that He is bringing, and being obedient where you need to be obedient.

—JOSHUA HARRIS, *Sex Is Not the Problem (Lust Is)*

Lord, help me to see the unique way
You provide for me as an escape from temptation.

THURSDAY

An Attitude of Grace

And you also were included in Christ when you heard the word of truth, the gospel of your salvation. Having believed, you were marked in him with a seal, the promised Holy Spirit, who is a deposit guaranteeing our inheritance until the redemption of those who are God's possession—to the praise of his glory.

Ephesians 1:13–14

We have a tendency to be unbalanced as we look at truth. We're told to speak the truth in love. What truth do people need to hear?

A person who doesn't know Jesus, for instance, needs to hear the truth. They need to be told that salvation is available to them in Christ. Part of that truth is the uncomfortable part—that they are going to hell for eternity if they don't know Jesus.

How do we in love convey that truth to someone? We have to start by taking an attitude of grace. We need to convey the truth so they understand that they need Jesus—but also that Jesus loves them and we do too.

—Randy Alcorn, *The Grace and Truth Paradox*

Lord, help me to develop discernment.

FRIDAY

Not in Vain

Why do the nations conspire and the peoples plot in vain? The kings of the earth take their stand and the rulers gather together against the Lord *and against his Anointed One. "Let us break their chains," they say, "and throw off their fetters." The One enthroned in heaven laughs; the Lord scoffs at them.*

Psalm 2:1–4

Scoffers have always mocked the doing of good. Scripture tells of God hearing them talking. They were saying, "What good is it to serve God? I mean, it's vain to serve God, because even the people who are ungodly seem to get away with everything."

Well, the Bible says that God heard them, but then He heard those who fear the Lord. "I want to write a book, a book of remembrance," said God, "about every single thing they have done. So on the day that they see Me, I will reward them."

So, my friend, the question is: What is God writing in the Book of Remembrance about you?

—Bruce Wilkinson, *A Life God Rewards*

Lord, help me not to lose heart,
to approach good works not as tedious but as joyful.

WEEKEND

Daily Dying to Self

But now, by dying to what once bound us, we have been released from the law so that we serve in the new way of the Spirit, and not in the old way of the written code.

Romans 7:6

If someone came up to me and said, "If you don't deny Christ, I'm going to shoot you," I don't think it would be that difficult to die for my faith at that point. What's difficult are the little things—the daily dying to self.

It's putting away my ego, my pride, my wants, my desires, my rights. That really is dying for my faith, and that's where it counts. And that's where it's hard, because I don't want to give up my rights. I don't want to give up my ego and my pride and my needs and my desires. I want to have it be all about me, instead of being all about God. That's really where it's hard to get up the nerve to die to self.

—Ryan Dobson, *2 Live 4*

Lord, help me to put my ego, pride, rights, and desires aside.

MONDAY

Behold the Lamb

The next day John saw Jesus coming toward him and said, "Look, the Lamb of God, who takes away the sin of the world! This is the one I meant when I said, 'A man who comes after me has surpassed me because he was before me.'"

John 1:29–30

One of the greatest qualities of any life is recognizing who God is and who we're not. Not unlike John the Baptist.

Imagine being the one God had chosen to baptize His Son. When John the Baptist saw Jesus coming, he uttered these amazing words: *"Look, the Lamb of God, who takes away the sin of the world!"* Imagine, all eyes were on John, and happily and gladly he pointed the eyes of everyone that day to the Savior.

John taught us the lesson of life. It's not bad to have attention placed on us. The joy of life, though, is in reflecting that attention back to the One who deserves it all, as we use our lives to draw the attention of people to the face of Jesus the source of life and forgiveness for all people.

—Louie Giglio, *I Am Not But I Know I Am*

Lord, help me to turn eyes to You.

TUESDAY

The Secret Place

None of the rulers of this age understood it, for if they had, they would not have crucified the Lord of glory. However, as it is written: "No eye has seen, no ear has heard, no mind has conceived what God has prepared for those who love him"—but God has revealed it to us by his Spirit. The Spirit searches all things, even the deep things of God.

1 Corinthians 2:8–10

It's more than a place of physical safety. It's more than a place of spiritual rest. The secret place is a place where you discern and discover the Lord's clear guidance through the illumination of His Word. It's where fragile ideas are free to mature.

What can God reveal to you in His secret place? The unimaginable. What eye has not seen nor ear heard. Treasures that are inconceivable to our eyes and hearts are the very things God has prepared for those who love Him.

Go to the secret place to seek God's plans for your life and be energized.

—J. Otis Ledbetter, *In the Secret Place*

Lord, help me to set aside time and energy to be with You in the secret place.

WEDNESDAY

First Things First

"But seek first his kingdom and his righteousness, and all these things will be given to you as well."

Matthew 6:33

Have you ever seen the performer spinning plates on poles? He spins one while the others slow down, and the whole time he works at figuring out which plate needs to be spun to keep the trick going.

Does your life ever feel like that? The only thing is, if you could pick the least important plates you might decide to drop a couple. Unfortunately, we typically treat all our plates all the same, and it's usually the most important plates that suffer.

We've all heard the phrase "first things first." But we don't always know what the first things are. Jesus tells us to seek first the kingdom and His righteousness. Take a little time to evaluate the plates you're spinning and focus on the true first things right now.

—Stuart Briscoe, *Time Bandits*

Lord, help me to identify Your "first things" that my life is in competition with.

THURSDAY

The Greatest Gift to a Child

But I have stilled and quieted my soul;
like a weaned child with its mother,
like a weaned child is my soul within me.

Psalm 131:2

Do you know what's the most valuable gift you could ever give a child?

No, it's probably not your old pickup, a college education, or maybe even your reputation. The most important gift you can ever give a child, whether or not you are a parent, is a relationship with you.

Over the years, I've had dozen of dates with my daughters and my sons. One with my daughter Ashley I'll never forget. We went out and we saw the movie *Bambi*. We went out to eat at a smorgasbord and had chocolate pudding and chocolate pie and chocolate milk. We had a blast together. And then when the evening ended, I asked Ashley what was the most important thing we'd done all evening. She said, "Just being with you, Dad."

Give your children the most important gift you'll ever give them: a relationship with you.

—Dennis and Barbara Rainey, *Growing a Spiritually Strong Family*

Lord, help me to spend time with
the important child in my life.

FRIDAY

Letter to God: Fear

You will keep in perfect peace
him whose mind is steadfast,
because he trusts in you.

Isaiah 26:3

Dear God,

Whenever I am afraid, help me trust You. Transform my fear, whatever its cause, into faith in You.

Lord, it seems like there are many reasons to fear, and I am sometimes overwhelmed. I fear for my family and my friends, my job and my life. The list feels endless. Yet I know that You don't want me to live a life driven by fear. You want me to rest in You. Remind me whose hand of protection is all around me. When my mind is spiraling out of control with concerns, give me the ability to turn from being a problem worrier to being a prayer warrior.

Let me walk through life knowing Your perfect peace, no matter what is happening around me.

Love,

Your princess, who is choosing trust in You over fear

—Sheri Rose Shepherd, *Prayers to My King*

WEEKEND

A Lot like Me

News about him spread all over Syria, and people brought to him all who were ill with various diseases, those suffering severe pain, the demon-possessed, those having seizures, and the paralyzed, and he healed them.

Matthew 4:24

People who end up in the margins of society aren't always just those you'd expect on the fringe, like the homeless or drug addicts. Instead, they're people a lot like you and a lot like me.

They can be people who have areas in their lives that are secret places they don't want to let anyone into. They might be the type who come to church and hear a sermon and have that repetitive theme going off in their head that if anyone really knew them, no one would love them.

People go to the margins so they can find solace, so they can find an opportunity to be protected from the reality of their sin, their pain. But out of that place Christ wants to invite you into His wholeness.

—Rick McKinley, *Jesus in the Margins*

Lord, help me to see the people in the margins as needing to be reminded that You love them.

MONDAY

The Fullness of the Spirit

This is what we speak, not in words taught us by human wisdom but in words taught by the Spirit, expressing spiritual truths in spiritual words. The man without the Spirit does not accept the things that come from the Spirit of God, for they are foolishness to him, and he cannot understand them, because they are spiritually discerned.... But we have the mind of Christ.

1 Corinithians 2:13–14, 16

In the Christian community today, there can be found the subtle idea that the fullness of the Spirit is reserved only for those who are called into ministry. Of course, according to the Bible that is not true. The Holy Spirit, who brings us to salvation, is provided for every believer.

But not only that, the Holy Spirit is our life. We cannot walk in our relationship with God without walking in the Spirit—that is, in harmony and in union with Him. Every believer has the opportunity to experience the fullness of the Holy Spirit.

—Henry and Mel Blackaby, *What's So Spiritual About Your Gifts?*

Lord, help me to walk closely with You in the Holy Spirit.

TUESDAY

The Judgment Seat of Christ

For we must all appear before the judgment seat of Christ, that each one may receive what is due him for the things done while in the body, whether good or bad.

2 Corinthians 5:10

One of the most glorious things about heaven is that there will be no tears. In fact, the Bible teaches that God will wipe away all tears. But do you know why He's going to have to wipe them away? It's because of something called the *bema*.

The bema means the judgment seat of Christ, and it takes place after you're already in heaven. At that moment, Jesus Christ is going to review your entire life. The Bible says one of two things will happen. Either Jesus will reward you, or you will suffer loss.

Make sure you live your life today so He won't have to lean across and wipe away your tears.

—Bruce Wilkinson, *A Life God Rewards*

Lord, help me to understand how to live now in a way that will make You pleased with me when I stand before You at the judgment seat.

WEDNESDAY

One Heart at a Time

Have mercy on me, O God, according to your unfailing love;
according to your great compassion blot out my transgressions.
Wash away all my iniquity and cleanse me from my sin.
Create in me a pure heart, O God,
and renew a steadfast spirit within me.
Do not cast me from your presence
or take your Holy Spirit from me.
Restore to me the joy of your salvation and
grant me a willing spirit, to sustain me.

Psalm 51:1–2, 10–12

It's time to press in, my friend.

Humble yourselves. Let the brightness and beauty of the holy presence of Jesus reveal how dependent you are upon His forgiveness and grace. Pray with every fiber of your being. Seek God's face above all else. Turn from all known sin. Pray with your fellow believers regularly and with your hearts in one accord. And finally, persevere in all things.

After all, when revival happens, it will happen one heart at a time.

—Pat Robertson, *Six Steps to Spiritual Revival*

Have mercy on me, O Lord,
and turn my heart to You today.

THURSDAY

After You've Blown It

Blessed is the man whose sin the Lord does not count against him and in whose spirit is no deceit.

Psalm 32:2

So what do you do after you've blown it? I remember speaking to a woman who had confessed the sins of her youth many times. I asked her how often she had confessed. She said, "Oh, at least a hundred times." I pointed out to her that once we confess our sins, God can be depended upon to be faithful and just to forgive us our sins.

We do not have to reconfess our sins. What we need to do is memorize Psalm 32! *How blessed is he whose transgression is forgiven and whose sin is covered.* We need to claim the forgiveness that God says we already have.

—Erwin Lutzer, *After You've Blown It*

Lord, thank You for forgiving my transgressions.

FRIDAY

God's Promptings

For you know that we dealt with each of you as a father deals with his own children, encouraging, comforting and urging you to live lives worthy of God, who calls you into his kingdom and glory. And we also thank God continually because, when you received the word of God, which you heard from us, you accepted it not as the word of men, but as it actually is, the word of God, which is at work in you who believe

1 Thessalonians 2:11–13

We see in the Scriptures that God sometimes sends visions and angels to communicate His will to individuals. But for believers today, the word *prompting* probably best describes how God's Spirit communicates with us in "the secret place."

Those promptings from the Lord are as real today as ever. It's in the secret place—where we're free from the world's distractions—where God can shine His light on His written Word in our hearts and make plain how it applies to our personal circumstances.

Go to the secret place to sense the genuine promptings of God's Spirit.

—J. Otis Ledbetter, *In the Secret Place*

Lord, help me to be receptive to Your communication.

WEEKEND

Fear Not

When I am afraid,
I will trust in you.
In God, whose word I praise,
in God I trust; I will not be afraid.
What can mortal man do to me?

Psalm 56:3–4

"God, what is wrong with me? Why do I feel this way? Are you still there for me?"

Pam: Years ago I saw a clever acrostic for the word *fear*. False Evidence Appearing Real. When we're in the middle of a situation where we're anxious or afraid, we start seeing mental pictures and thinking things not necessarily part of reality. A lot of our anxieties come from the tendency to overestimate the probability of a harmful event.

Steve: It amazes me, as I go through Scripture, how many times it says, "Fear not." So my challenge is to say, "Okay, Lord, I'm going to let go of these fears because I really am not in control anyway. God is the only One who is in control."

—Dr. Steve Stephens & Pam Vredevelt, *The Wounded Woman*

Lord, help me to turn my fear over to You.

MONDAY

On Respect

Then they can train the younger women to love their husbands and children, to be self-controlled and pure, to be busy at home, to be kind, and to be subject to their husbands, so that no one will malign the word of God..

Titus 2:4–5

One of the most fundamental truths about men, believe it or not, is that if they had to, they would rather feel respected than loved by the woman in their life. Women most want to feel loved and cherished. So women assume the same for the men in their lives. They say, "Honey, I love you," and do things they hope their husbands will perceive as loving. At the same time, they criticize them, question their decisions, and tease them in public. The man will think, *She just doesn't respect me. She doesn't trust me.* And therefore he won't feel loved.

If women want the key to the hearts of men, they need to demonstrate that respect and trust and then watch them light up.

—Shaunti Feldhahn, *For Women Only*

Lord, help me to be supportive of marriage, of married couples, and of those important people in my own life, for Your sake.

TUESDAY

The Foreverness of Time

"Can you bind the beautiful Pleiades?
Can you loose the cords of Orion?
Can you bring forth the constellations in their seasons
or lead out the Bear with its cubs?
Do you know the laws of the heavens?
Can you set up God's dominion over the earth?"

JOB 38:31–33

When I think about God and I think about forever and I think about eternity, my brain just freezes. I can't fathom timelessness. We live in time and that's the way we are. When you're young, and I still am, you think you'll live forever. But then you get a concept of time, and you realize exactly how short this life is. You gain a concept of eternity in the foreverness of time. And it just makes you cling to Him even tighter.

It draws me close to God. He wants us to be with Him forever in eternity.

—CHRIS TOMLIN, *The Way I Was Made*

Lord, thank You for reaching into time to save me.

WEDNESDAY

His Undivided Attention

I love the Lord, for he heard my voice;
he heard my cry for mercy.
Because he turned his ear to me,
I will call on him as long as I live.

Psalm 116:1–2

You've been there. You're going through a period of heartache and you want to talk it over with a friend. But the phone call is interrupted or never returned. Or worse, you're talking with a friend, and there's very little eye contact and few words. You get the impression that the friend is only half listening.

That may be the loneliest part of loneliness, knowing that no one really understands or even cares what you're going through. But thankfully Jesus has been through it too. He knows what it feels like to have friends who don't always care. And He listens; He is not distracted; His eye contact never falters. His heart is with yours in the middle of your pain.

—Joni Eareckson Tada, *31 Days to Intimacy with God*

Lord, thank You for being my constant companion.

THURSDAY

Serving He Who Rewards

Whatever you do, work at it with all your heart, as working for the Lord, not for men, since you know that you will receive an inheritance from the Lord as a reward. It is the Lord Christ you are serving.

Colossians 3:23–24

The eleventh chapter of the book of Hebrews is called the faith chapter in the Bible. The most important verse in that chapter is 6: "And without faith it is impossible to please God, because anyone who comes to him must believe that he exists and that he rewards those who earnestly seek him."

Some translations use the word *rewarder*. Do you know what that word *rewarder* literally means in the language it was written in? It means that you must believe that God is the One who will pay you back your wages for working with Him. Just think about it. You can't please God unless you believe He's a rewarder.

—Bruce Wilkinson, *A Life God Rewards*

Lord, help me to believe that You see my work on earth and are guiding me to accomplish Your purposes.

FRIDAY

Love Is Patient

1 Corinthians 13:1–7

If I speak in the tongues of men and of angels, but have not love,
I am only a resounding gong or a clanging cymbal.
If I have the gift of prophecy and can fathom all mysteries and all knowledge,
and if I have a faith that can move mountains,
but have not love, I am nothing.
If I give all I possess to the poor and surrender my body to the flames,
but have not love, I gain nothing.

Love is patient, love is kind.
It does not envy, it does not boast, it is not proud.
It is not rude, it is not self-seeking, it is not easily angered,
it keeps no record of wrongs.
Love does not delight in evil but rejoices with the truth.
It always protects, always trusts, always hopes, always perseveres.

Lord, thank You for the gift of love.

WEEKEND

Love Never Fails

1 Corinthians 13:8–13

Love never fails. But where there are prophecies,
they will cease; where there are tongues, they will be stilled;
where there is knowledge, it will pass away.
For we know in part and we prophesy in part,
but when perfection comes, the imperfect disappears.
When I was a child, I talked like a child, I thought
like a child, I reasoned like a child.
When I became a man, I put childish ways behind me.
Now we see but a poor reflection as in a mirror;
then we shall see face to face.
Now I know in part; then I shall know fully,
even as I am fully known.

And now these three remain: faith, hope and love.
But the greatest of these is love.

Lord, thank You for the opportunity to grow in love.

MONDAY

Truth and Grace

“[…]od so loved the world that he gave his one and only Son, that whoever […]es in him shall not perish but have eternal life. For God did not send his Son into the world to condemn the world, but to save the world through him.”

JOHN 3:16–17

Jesus found a way to be filled perfectly with both grace and truth. What that means is you never compromise truth, but on the other hand you don't necessarily condemn people when they fall short.

It's like a scene in court, where a judge reviews a case before him. There stands the judge's son, facing serious charges. The judge finds him guilty and sentences him to the maximum penalty. Then he takes off his robe, comes around the bench, hugs his son, and takes his punishment on himself.

Grace recognizes what truth is and sees when people fall short. But grace also steps in and pays the price. Grace comes alongside people and helps them to arrive where God wants them to be.

—RICHARD BLACKABY, *Putting a Face on Grace*

Lord, thank You for being both Judge and Savior.

TUESDAY

Letter to God: New Creation

Therefore, if anyone is in Christ, he is a new creation; the old has gone, the new has come!

2 Corinthians 5:17

Dear God,

Your Word teaches that I am a new creation, that I am not the same person I was before I met You, and that the old me is gone. I want to believe that, but I need Your help.

Please show me how to live as the new person You have made me. I want to be the princess You have created me to be. Show me the people and things I need to walk away from so I can walk more closely with You. Wash me white as snow. Put in me a clean heart—a heart that longs for Your love and approval.

Trusting in Your faithfulness, I thank You for what You're doing in me, and I thank You for what I will become. Thank You for giving Your life to pay the price for my sin. Thank You that the Holy Spirit's power that raised You from the dead is in me, a new creation.

Love,

Your princess, who is a new creation

—Sheri Rose Shepherd, *Prayers to My King*

WEDNESDAY

THE VISIBLE AND THE INVISIBLE

For our struggle is not against flesh and blood, but against the rulers, against the authorities, against the powers of this dark world and against the spiritual forces of evil in the heavenly realms.

EPHESIANS 6:12

There is a massive connection between what's happening in our world and the spiritual battle we face. Why? Because everything visible and spiritual is influenced or controlled by something invisible and spiritual.

So for instance, the breakdown of happiness in people's lives is because of the camouflage of what true happiness really is. The breakdown of family is because of deception about what marriage is. An illegitimate definition has been ascribed to realities like drugs and sex, causing distance from God.

The only solution is spiritual warfare. To fix the visible you've got to deal with the invisible.

—TONY EVANS, *God Can Not Be Trusted*

Lord, help me to fight against the forces of evil in my life.

THURSDAY

No Watering Down

And this is my prayer: that your love may abound more and more in knowledge and depth of insight, so that you may be able to discern what is best and may be pure and blameless until the day of Christ, filled with the fruit of righteousness that comes through Jesus Christ—to the glory and praise of God.

PHILIPPIANS 1:9–11

We tend to water down truth, don't we? When we do, we also end up watering down grace. When truth and grace are watered down, they become just another version of what the world is talking about.

But God's truth is transforming and God's grace is transforming. Truth and grace, when they're at work in a heart, transform us. We become different people. And that's where you can tell the difference between what the world calls truth and grace and what Jesus calls truth and grace—the truth and grace Jesus was full of.

We have to be sure that we're speaking in God's truth *and* in God's grace.

—RANDY ALCORN, *The Grace and Truth Paradox*

Lord, help me to make a stand for truth, but in a loving way.

FRIDAY

How to Keep Your Money

"Do not store up for yourselves treasures on earth, where moth and rust destroy, and where thieves break in and steal. But store up for yourselves treasures in heaven, where moth and rust do not destroy, and where thieves do not break in and steal. For where your treasure is, there your heart will be also."

Matthew 6:19–21

The vast majority of people I know misunderstand what Jesus taught about money.

They think Jesus wants you to lose your money. But the truth of it is He doesn't want you to lose a cent. He instructed you to lay up "for yourselves"—not for someone else, for you—treasures in heaven. Moths and rust and thieves can't get to it there.

Jesus doesn't want you to lose your money; He wants you to keep it. But you must pass it on. You must give it away now to keep it.

—Bruce Wilkinson, *A Life God Rewards*

Lord, help me to have the right perspective about finances and to always seek to serve You with my money.

WEEKEND

Praying Together

In the same way, the Spirit helps us in our weakness. We do not know what we ought to pray for, but the Spirit himself intercedes for us with groans that words cannot express.

Romans 8:26

What's the single best piece of advice for a young couple?

The best advice we ever received, which we pass on every chance we get, is to pray every day with your spouse, girlfriend, or boyfriend.

We've been doing this since 1972, and there is no other spiritual discipline in our lives that has brought us closer together as a couple and to God than by praying together. We've prayed about our problems. We've prayed about our successes. We've given thanks in all things. We've asked God for wisdom.

Prayer together as a couple will change the course of your relationship and your family.

—Dennis and Barbara Rainey, *Growing a Spiritually Strong Family*

Lord, thank You for the privilege of prayer.

MONDAY

Inside Story

Each one of you also must love his wife as he loves himself,
and the wife must respect her husband.

Ephesians 5:33

Women think men look confident, but on the inside, many of them are secretly vulnerable and insecure. They go through life feeling like, "I'm really not sure I know exactly what I'm doing, and I hope nobody finds out." This feeling shows up not just at work. It can be worse at home. As one man said, "At least at work I have some idea whether I'm doing a good job. How do I know whether I'm doing a good job as a husband or as a father? The only measurement is the happiness of my wife."

Women need to realize their enormous opportunity to learn their husbands' needs and to build them up and support them in the way they most need. One of the best ways of doing that is realizing that they need affirmation.

—Shaunti Feldhahn, *For Women Only*

Lord, help me to be as affirming as I can.

TUESDAY

No Pipe Dream

"Here is my servant whom I have chosen, the one I love, in whom I delight; I will put my Spirit on him, and he will proclaim justice to the nations."

MATTHEW 12:18

We may make think that God exists to bless America, but according to Scripture, America exists to bless God.

Suppose God's glory became our priority and our prayer. Suppose our elected officials daily asked, "How can we honor God in our decisions? How can the school introduce students to God? How can this army promote the name of God?" You say, "You're pipe dreaming, Max. We have legislators who disavow Scripture and mock morality. We can't make a nation exist for the glory of God."

And you're right. But God can, and He will if we ask Him.

—MAX LUCADO, *Turn*

Lord, help me to seek Your glory through praying for our nation.

WEDNESDAY

The Good Fight

A married woman is concerned about the affairs of this world—how she can please her husband.

1 Corinthians 7:34

In the movie *Rocky*, the main character wanted to be a boxer, but he couldn't without his wife's support and confidence in him. It is impossible for women to overestimate how much men depend on their wives' belief in them. Or how insecure they feel when that belief is absent.

One man said, "I go out and feel like I fight the good fight every day in the ring. And it's very lonely. That's why when I come home, I want my wife to be there in my corner and to massage my shoulders and to tell me, 'Thank you, honey. You are doing such a good job.'"

Women need to understand how much men need that affirmation.

—Shaunti Feldhahn, *For Women Only*

Lord, thank You for your affirmation of Your children, and help me to be that positive person You've designed me to be.

THURSDAY

Unconditional Mercy

"Come to me, all you who are weary and burdened, and I will give you rest. Take my yoke upon you and learn from me, for I am gentle and humble in heart, and you will find rest for your souls."

Matthew 11:28–29

In 2003, college students Mike Yankoski and Sam Purvis spent more than five months living on the streets of America to learn what it means to be homeless.

When we got to Washington DC, we needed to start panhandling in order to survive. We didn't have any money. It was humiliating. It showed me a little bit of what unconditional love from Jesus Christ is.

When a person would reach out to us and even just have a conversation with us and imply *you are a human being made in the image of God*, that's an indication of what Jesus does Himself when He reaches out to us in the Father's love and says, "Come to me, all you who are weary. I will give you rest." That's mercy. When someone would maybe even give us their whole takeout bag of food from a restaurant, that was mercy manifest. We felt that. We knew that. We experienced that.

—Mike Yankoski, *Under the Overpass*

Lord, help me to treat everyone as if they were You.

FRIDAY

Nothing Counterfeit

Keep to a path far from [the adulteress], do not go near the door of her house, lest you give your best strength to others and your years to one who is cruel.... For a man's ways are in full view of the Lord, and he examines all his paths.

Proverbs 5:8–9, 21

A man once told me that he worked in an office with many attractive women. One day, as he was walking down the hall, a young lady was walking towards him, and he looked down at the ground and said a prayer in his heart. He said, "God, why did You have to make women so beautiful? Why did You make this woman so beautiful?" He felt the Lord speak to him and say, "I made her beautiful for her husband."

That story was a reminder that God has given us our sexuality in the good gift of marriage. God has made something so wonderful for those of us who are called to be married. We need to delight in that and turn away from the counterfeits.

—Joshua Harris, *Sex Is Not the Problem (Lust Is)*

Lord, help me to keep my sexuality sacred.

WEEKEND

Larger than Life

Jesus entered the temple area and drove out all who were buying and selling there. He overturned the tables of the money changers and the benches of those selling doves.

MATTHEW 21:12

When you think of Jesus, do you think of statues and halos, of stuffy religious ceremony? When you open the pages of Scripture, you see a picture of a Jesus who is larger than life.

The first miracle Jesus performed was a wedding where He changed water into wine for a bunch of people who had already been at the party for a weeklong festivity. (If a pastor today showed up at a party with 180 gallons of wine, he'd probably lose his job!)

We want to clean Jesus up rather than proclaim the radical nature of His love and the radical ways in which He expressed that love to people who need. The great hope here is that that kind of love is the way that He loves you.

—RICK MCKINLEY, *Jesus in the Margins*

Lord, help me to love radically also.

MONDAY

Perish the Thought

All of us also lived among them at one time, gratifying the cravings of our sinful nature and following its desires and thoughts. Like the rest, we were by nature objects of wrath. But because of his great love for us, God, who is rich in mercy, made us alive with Christ even when we were dead in transgressions—it is by grace you have been saved.

EPHESIANS 2:3–5

"For God so loved the world that he gave his only begotten Son, that whoever believes in him shall not perish." Death is at the very foundation of that statement—eternal death. A destiny that by our own efforts is inescapable.

Humanly speaking, none of us has an eternal hope of anything except to perish. Yet this inescapable fact brought a response from God's heart. Something about the word *perish* made the Cross eternally necessary with no other effective strategy being possible.

He so loved the world that He gave His only Son so we would not perish.

—HENRY BLACKABY, *Experiencing the Cross*

Lord, thank you for Your gift of eternal life.

TUESDAY

Heaven Is Not a Choir

"In the time of those kings, the God of heaven will set up a kingdom that will never be destroyed, nor will it be left to another people. It will crush all those kingdoms and bring them to an end, but it will itself endure forever."

DANIEL 2:44

I can remember sitting in church as a young man and the pastor preaching about heaven. And I can remember saying to myself, *I don't want to go to heaven. I mean, not right now. There are too many things in my life I want to do.*

To me, life on earth was more attractive than life in heaven. Do you know why? Because all I could think about heaven was that I would be sitting in a choir, singing all the time. When God made Adam and Eve, He didn't put them in a choir, did He? Instead He put them in a world.

Ladies and gentlemen, heaven is not a choir. It is going to be a place far more exhilarating and pleasurable than anything you and I could ever imagine.

—BRUCE WILKINSON, *A Life God Rewards*

Lord, help me to learn more about what heaven is and how it impacts my life on earth.

WEDNESDAY

Our Best

Blessed is the man who finds wisdom, the man who gains understanding,
for she is more profitable than silver and yields better returns than gold.
She is more precious than rubies; nothing you desire can compare with her.
Long life is in her right hand; in her left hand are riches and honor....
She is a tree of life to those who embrace her; those who lay hold of her will be blessed.

PROVERBS 3:13–16, 18

Wives need to trust their husbands and not always assume that their way of doing things is the right way. For instance, repeatedly asking, "Have you done it yet?" is probably not a big deal. But inherent in that question is the assumption that men need the reminder, that they're either incapable of remembering on their own, or that they can remember but need prodding to do the job. What they are hearing is, *I don't trust you.*

Instead, what if women were to proactively assume the best of the men in their lives instead of the worst? For example, *I asked him to do it. He hasn't done it. I trust my husband, therefore there is a reason he hasn't done it.* Let's look at our assumptions and maybe believe that men actually deserve our best.

—SHAUNTI FELDHAHN, *For Women Only*

Lord, help me to better trust the important people in my life.

THURSDAY

ENTRY-LEVEL CHRISTIANITY

You then, my son, be strong in the grace that is in Christ Jesus. And the things you have heard me say in the presence of many witnesses entrust to reliable men who will also be qualified to teach others.... Reflect on what I am saying, for the Lord will give you insight into all this. Remember Jesus Christ, raised from the dead, descended from David. This is my gospel, for which I am suffering even to the point of being chained like a criminal. But God's word is not chained. Therefore I endure everything for the sake of the elect, that they too may obtain the salvation that is in Christ Jesus, with eternal glory.

2 TIMOTHY 2:1–2,7–10

Christians have a tendency to "move on" from the gospel, as if it is an entry-level message of Christianity. Even Paul, obviously aware of the tendency to forget, reminds Timothy to remember Jesus Christ!

In fact, "we never move on from the cross, only into a more profound understanding of the cross."*

—C. J. MAHANEY, *The Cross-Centered Life*

Lord, help me to never take the gospel for granted.

*David Prior, *Message of 1 Corinthians: Life in the Local Church* (Downers Grove, IL: InterVarsity Press, 1985), 51.

FRIDAY

Scrooge's Second Chance

I will give you a new heart and put a new spirit in you; I will remove from you your heart of stone and give you a heart of flesh. And I will put my Spirit in you and move you to follow my decrees and be careful to keep my laws.

Ezekiel 36:26–27

I was rereading Charles Dickens's classic story *A Christmas Carol*. It's the familiar story of Ebenezer Scrooge. At the beginning, he's wealthy but miserable. He's caustic, always complaining, and of course, horrendously greedy. But then, after his encounters with the three spirits on Christmas Day, he's given a second chance at life.

On the story's final page, after Ebenezer Scrooge becomes a man of eternal perspective, Dickens says this of Scrooge:

> Some people laughed to see the alteration in him. But he let them laugh and little heeded them.... His own heart laughed: and that was quite enough for him. And it was always said of him, that he knew how to keep Christmas well, if any man alive possessed the knowledge.

Ebenezer Scrooge becomes a man of eternal perspective.

—Randy Alcorn, *The Treasure Principle*

Lord, help my heart to laugh with generosity because of Your generous Spirit.

WEEKEND

We Proclaim

1 John 1:1–7

That which was from the beginning, which we have heard,
which we have seen with our eyes,
which we have looked at and our hands have touched—
this we proclaim concerning the Word of life.
The life appeared; we have seen it and testify to it,
and we proclaim to you the eternal life, which was with the Father
and has appeared to us. We proclaim to you what we have seen and heard,
so that you also may have fellowship with us.
And our fellowship is with the Father and with his Son, Jesus Christ.
We write this to make our joy complete.

This is the message we have heard from him and declare to you:
God is light; in him there is no darkness at all.
If we claim to have fellowship with him
yet walk in the darkness, we lie and do not live by the truth.
But if we walk in the light, as he is in the light,
we have fellowship with one another,
and the blood of Jesus, his Son, purifies us from all sin.

Lord, thank You for Your light.

MONDAY

Beyond the Wedding Day

In fact, though by this time you ought to be teachers, you need someone to teach you the elementary truths of God's word all over again. You need milk, not solid food! Anyone who lives on milk, being still an infant, is not acquainted with the teaching about righteousness.

HEBREWS 5:12–13

The day I got married was a great day. It was on the beach. We walked down an aisle bordered by surfboards. All my family and friends were there. It was a fantastic day.

But I'm not still sitting there on the beach saying, "What a great wedding day we had." You have to move on. The marriage is not about your wedding day. The marriage is about the journey you take with another person, learning about them, growing, stretching, compromising, loving that person more and more every day.

And in the same way, Christianity isn't about the day I became a Christian. I've got to have a journey with Christ and learn and grow and love Him more every day and try to bring more people on that journey. That's what Christianity is really about.

—RYAN DOBSON, *2 Live 4*

Lord, help me to seek more spiritual meat.

TUESDAY

Letter to God: Rest

My soul finds rest in God alone;
my salvation comes from him.

Psalm 62:1

Dear God,

I am so tired, physically, emotionally, and spiritually. Please help me rest in Your arms right now.

Help me to gain Your perspective on my life. Father, I can't keep up the pace that my daily to-do list requires. I know You didn't call me to a crazy, filled-up life that is out of control, so I come to You and confess that I can't do it all. And I don't want to try anymore. Help me, Lord, not to feel guilty when I sit at Your feet a little while each day, or when I obey Your command to take a day of rest each week.

Help me break free from the bondage of busyness and enter into a life of peace and divine purpose.

Love,

Your princess, who loves You and longs to rest in You

—Sheri Rose Shepherd, *Prayers to My King*

WEDNESDAY

Out of Focus

Now the serpent was more crafty than any of the wild animals the LORD God had made. He said to the woman, "Did God really say, 'You must not eat from any tree in the garden'?"

GENESIS 3:1

Satan wants to get us to believe that God is holding out on us. He wants us to believe that serving our self-interest over serving God is the way to go. The way he does that is by making God's restrictions seem so big that by comparison His allowances seem small.

Adam and Eve were permitted every tree in the Garden of Eden except one. Satan focused on that one. He made it loom so large that they missed out all the other trees they could have been enjoying.

That's why he will take one thing in your life that is a restriction and make it seem like the only thing in your life. Beware, lest you miss the goodness of God.

—TONY EVANS, *God Can Not Be Trusted*

Lord, forgive me for thinking that You might hold out on me.

THURSDAY

Blessings Never Run Out

Grace and peace to you from God our Father and the Lord Jesus Christ. Praise be to the God and Father of our Lord Jesus Christ, who has blessed us in the heavenly realms with every spiritual blessing in Christ. For he chose us in him before the creation of the world to be holy and blameless in his sight.

Ephesians 1:2–4

You got up at six o'clock in the morning on the nose. And you went to the place where you love to sit and meet God and pray. And you said, "God, would You please bless me indeed? Would You pour out Your kindness and goodness upon me?" And God turned around and said to you, "You know, dear one, I wish I could, but the problem is this guy Wilkinson was here at 5:59, and he asked me to bless him and I did. And I'm sorry, but there are just no more blessings left for you."

Is that the way it works? Of course not. There's an unlimited number of blessings, because when you ask, God makes them on the spot for you. So never again wonder if you should ask for a blessing. They'll never run out.

—Bruce Wilkinson, *Beyond Jabez*

Lord, help me to remember that Your generosity, like Your love, is infinite.

FRIDAY

Abiding Forever

In the beginning was the Word, and the Word was with God, and the Word was God.

John 1:1

Buddhism prides itself in the fact that everything is impermanent. Nothing ultimately lasts. Your *self* is impermanent, matter around you is impermanent, the world itself ultimately dissolves. We use the analogy of a candle being extinguished. It is just the extinguishing of the self where there is no ultimate further desire. Everything is impermanent.

However, Jesus told us that the Word of God abides forever. He said His Word cannot be broken. And that we will dwell with Him forever in an eternal dwelling place, which He calls heaven. So the truth is, with Him life is eternal and permanent.

—Ravi Zacharias, *The Lotus and the Cross*

Lord, help me to dwell in You through the Word.

WEEKEND

Getting Our Attention

Do not hold against us the sins of the fathers;
may your mercy come quickly to meet us,
for we are in desperate need.
Help us, O God our Savior, for the glory of your name;
deliver us and forgive our sins for your name's sake

PSALM 79:8–9

A man named Ryan had given his wife the AIDS virus. She understandably was very angry with him. He in turn was very angry with himself and filled with self-condemnation. He said to me, "Show me that there is a way out, or else I'll blow my brains out."

I pointed out to him that there is hope for all sinners. But I also told him that he had one good thing going for him—God finally had his attention.

We all have to come to the end of ourselves before we desperately begin to seek God. So, my friend, I want you to know that whatever mess you're in today may be God's message to you to turn to Him in repentance and faith.

—ERWIN LUTZER, *After You've Blown It*

Lord, you have my attention!
I will follow you!

MONDAY

The Gift

There are different kinds of gifts, but the same Spirit. There are different kinds of service, but the same Lord. There are different kinds of working, but the same God works all of them in all men. Now to each one the manifestation of the Spirit is given for the common good.

1 Corinthians 12:4–7

Some Christians seek the gifts of the Spirit. However, according Scripture that really is the wrong pursuit.

According to 1 Corinthians 12:7, the Spirit manifests Himself to every member for the common good. *The Spirit* is the Gift, and when God gives an assignment to an individual or a church, the Holy Spirit is present to equip them to do it. He does not distribute gifts so that we can use them as we want to.

He is the Gift, and He manifests His own presence in the life of the individual who's on assignment from God.

—Henry and Mel Blackaby, *What's So Spiritual About Your Gifts?*

Lord, thank You for the gift of Your Spirit.

TUESDAY

WHOSE STANDARDS?

Therefore, I urge you, brothers, in view of God's mercy, to offer your bodies as living sacrifices, holy and pleasing to God—this is your spiritual act of worship. Do not conform any longer to the pattern of this world, but be transformed by the renewing of your mind. Then you will be able to test and approve what God's will is—his good, pleasing and perfect will.

ROMANS 12:1–2

When it comes to our media habits, our standards have to be directed by God's Word.

We need to mind His standards, not a rating some association came up with. I appreciate the watchdogs, but we have to answer before God for what we watch and what those scenes and those images lead to in our own hearts. We need to exercise a level of discernment and ask the question, "Does the story, does the content of this movie, lead to something that I can thank God for?"

Our standards have to be based on what Scripture says is glorifying to our Lord.

—JOSHUA HARRIS, *Sex Is Not the Problem (Lust Is)*

Lord, help me to keep Your Word foremost in my mind as I encounter media choices.

WEDNESDAY

For the Children

Train a child in the way he should go,
and when he is old he will not turn from it.

Proverbs 22:6

Do you know how to develop a relationship with the children in your life? Whether you're a parent or not, you can help a child endure just about anything by following these three steps.

Number one, give the child your time. Play catch, read a book together, or just hang out with them. Secondly, touch. If you haven't hugged the child in your life recently, give them a giant bear hug. Regular hugs and kisses and holding hands all say, "You know what? I love you. You're special." And finally, talk to your child. Share your values, your expectations, goals, and dreams for them. And then listen to theirs about their own life. Ask them about what's troubling them and how you can best serve them in accomplishing their objectives.

All of these things build a relationship with your children, which can help them endure many a storm.

—Dennis and Barbara Rainey, *Growing a Spiritually Strong Family*

Lord, help me to make children an inviolate priority.

THURSDAY

Good, Not Harm

A wife of noble character who can find?
She is worth far more than rubies.
Her husband has full confidence in her
and lacks nothing of value.
She brings him good, not harm,
all the days of her life.

PROVERBS 31:10–12

How does a woman show a man respect? One way is to be careful about conveying the opposite.

Let me give you a silly example. Most women have been in the situation where a boyfriend, husband, or brother is driving in circles and refusing to stop and ask for directions. When they say, "Honey, please just stop and ask for directions," what the man is hearing is, "I don't trust you." So this is a choice. Let's choose to trust the man in our lives and convey to him that he is more important to us than anything else in the world.

—SHAUNTI FELDHAHN, *For Women Only*

Lord, help me to ask You for directions when I need them and to follow Your instructions when it comes to building up the important people in my life.

FRIDAY

"God, Please Send Me"

From inside the fish Jonah prayed to the Lord his God. He said: "In my distress I called to the Lord, and he answered me. From the depths of the grave I called for help, and you listened to my cry."

Jonah 2:1–2

A group of directors, actors, and producers asked me to come speak to them on *The Prayer of Jabez.* They were having a difficult time believing that a religious book was number one in America at the time.

When I got to part two of the prayer (*Would you please expand my territory?*), I said, "How many of you, at least one time in your life, knew that God asked you to go over and help someone else and you said, 'No'?" Everyone raised their hand. Then I said to them, "Could it be, then, that when a person comes along to God and says, 'God, would You please send me,' God says, 'Yes,'?"

"Therefore," I said, "If you want to watch God intervene in your life, just look up toward heaven and say, 'God, please send me.'"

—Bruce Wilkinson, *Beyond Jabez*

Lord, help me to remember that You have called me and equipped me as Your servant.

WEEKEND

Friend of Sinners

"For John came neither eating nor drinking, and they say,
'He has a demon.' The Son of Man came eating and drinking, and they say,
'Here is a glutton and a drunkard, a friend of tax collectors and "sinners."'
But wisdom is proved right by her actions."

Matthew 11:18–19

The Pharisees, the religious people during Jesus' time, tried to demean Jesus by giving Him the title *friend of sinners*. But in the heart of God, it was actually the greatest title you could give the Savior of the world. Because for you and me, as sinners, that title means Jesus is here to invite us to friendship.

The greatest picture of the grace of God is that the purest, most holy person in the world was willing to rub up next to people, who desperately need forgiveness, and in that place to offer them friendship.

—Rick McKinley, *Jesus in the Margins*

Lord, help me to remember that like Christ
I am a friend of sinners.

MONDAY

Letter to God: Chosen

We are therefore Christ's ambassadors, as though God were making his appeal through us. We implore you on Christ's behalf: Be reconciled to God.

2 Corinthians 5:20

Dear God,

It's so hard for me to believe that You chose me to represent You to the world. Lord, I feel so inadequate to be called Your princess. I want to be what You called me to be, but I don't know how. I need You to help me let go of who I think I am and become who You say I am.

I know that You have given me a free will and that you would never force me to live for You. Yet I want to be totally devoted to You. I want to leave my life as a legacy. I'm asking You today to anoint me and show me how to live and act as Your princess.

Because You chose me, I choose to follow You today. I love You and I feel privileged to call You the Lord of my life and my Savior.

Love,

Your princess, who says yes

—Sheri Rose Shepherd, *Prayers to My King*

TUESDAY

Broken Hearts

I cry to you, O Lord;
I say, "You are my refuge,
my portion in the land of the living."
Listen to my cry,
for I am in desperate need;
rescue me from those who pursue me,
for they are too strong for me.

Psalm 142:5–6

All of us at some point in life will be able to realize the statement that God is enough. Why? Because all of us at some point in life will be broken, and the realization that God is enough happens in our brokenness.

At the very hard times of life is when we find that God is enough. That His grace is enough to sustain us. God doesn't desire our sacrifices; he desires our broken hearts.

That's when we know that He's enough for us.

—Chris Tomlin, *The Way I Was Made*

Lord, help me to believe that You are enough.

WEDNESDAY

Blessings and Prosperity

You will eat the fruit of your labor; blessings and prosperity will be yours.
Your wife will be like a fruitful vine within your house;
your sons will be like olive shoots around your table.
Thus is the man blessed who fears the Lord.

Psalm 128:2–4

Women may not realize the power they hold to either build men up, or to tear them down.

I was speaking at a large church one Sunday. The pastor, a very popular Christian leader, was explaining this to his congregation. He stood up in front of his congregation and he said, "I know you all think you have a good pastor. You don't. You have a great pastor's wife."

There are a lot of great men out there who are mediocre simply because their wives will not support them and help them reach greatness. And there are a lot of mediocre men who are becoming great men because their wives love and support them. Let's not underestimate the incredible importance women have on the life of men, to build them up or to tear them down.

—Shaunti Feldhahn, *For Women Only*

Lord, help me to seek greatness for Your glory.

THURSDAY

Wounded by the Word

For the word of God is living and active. Sharper than any double-edged sword, it penetrates even to dividing soul and spirit, joints and marrow; it judges the thoughts and attitudes of the heart.

Hebrews 4:12

You've read the verse in the Bible many times and never had it affect you. Then you glance at it and *zap*, it hits you. The Spirit's intrusion. Sometimes we welcome it. Other times it brings a groan or even tears. We've been wounded by the Word of God.

Andrew Murray puts it this way. Jesus has no tenderness toward anything that is ultimately going to ruin a person in service to Him. If God brings to your mind a verse that hurts you, you may be sure there is something He wants to hurt. If there is anything in your life that grieves the Spirit of God, you won't be able to find the intimacy with Him your heart desires. Ask the Searcher of hearts to make you aware of anything that hinders your relationship with Him.

—Joni Eareckson Tada, *31 Days to Intimacy with God*

Lord, help me to let Your Word cut through my resistance to Your changes in my life.

FRIDAY

On the Front Lines

Put on the full armor of God so that you can take your stand against the devil's schemes.

Ephesians 6:11

A modern-day war scene:

"I.T.—Jenkins here."

"Jenkins! Our computers are locked up. Get your team down here—quick! We're fighting a war here!"

Or maybe this is closer to your reality: "Bankers, stand your post! Sven, James, follow me—go, go, go!"

Whether we recognize it or not, if we're part of the kingdom of God, we're all on the front lines. Too often, though, that's just an abstract thought, not a reality. See, the choices we make and the priorities we set can have long-lasting implications. When we don't see the kingdom for what it really is, we just coast and haphazardly set priorities. At best, this leads to disappointment. At worst, disaster.

By aligning everything under the most important thing, the kingdom, we'll get through more battles with fewer wounds.

—Stuart Briscoe, *Time Bandits*

Lord, help me to prepare for spiritual warfare.

WEEKEND

In the Beginning

John 1:1–5, 10–14

In the beginning was the Word, and the Word was with God,
and the Word was God. He was with God in the beginning.
Through him all things were made; without him nothing was made
that has been made. In him was life, and that life was the light of men.
The light shines in the darkness, but the darkness has not understood it....
He was in the world, and though the world was made through him, the world
did not recognize him. He came to that which was his own, but his own
did not receive him. Yet to all who received him, to those who believed in his
name, he gave the right to become children of God—children born not of
natural descent, nor of human decision or a husband's will,
but born of God. The Word became flesh and made his dwelling among us.
We have seen his glory, the glory of the One and Only,
who came from the Father, full of grace and truth.

Lord, thank You for dwelling among us.

MONDAY

What It Cost God

This is how we know what love is: Jesus Christ laid down his life for us. And we ought to lay down our lives for our brothers.

1 John 3:16

We sometimes forget what it cost God to forgive us. Sometimes we act as if the cross was for big sinners like murderers and tyrants. We minimize our own need of forgiveness. But for even just one of our sins, the Son of God would have had to die on the cross in the same painful, excruciating manner. And because of that, we should never lose the wonder of the fact that God paid the price to forgive us. We didn't deserve it. We did nothing to earn it. There is no way to pay Him back. He just forgave us because He loves us, because He knew we couldn't restore the relationship with Him on our own.

When we really understand what it cost God to forgive us, we ought to be the most forgiving people there are.

—Richard Blackaby, *Putting a Face on Grace*

Lord, help me to lay down my life daily for others.

TUESDAY

BLESSINGS OF THE HEART

Give ear to my words, O LORD, consider my sighing.
Listen to my cry for help, my King and my God, for to you I pray.
In the morning, O LORD, you hear my voice;
in the morning I lay my requests before you and wait in expectation.

PSALM 5:1–3

When you ask God, "Would You please bless me indeed?" do you realize that's all that you ask? You're not saying to Him, "Please bless me in this way or in this time." You're not asking Him to give you anything, except a blessing.

And do you realize that blessing takes place inside your heart? It's a response that your heart has to something that occurred. That's why you can find many wealthy people who are anything but blessed, and you can find many poor people who are filled with blessing.

Therefore, when you ask God to bless you, you are recognizing that He has the freedom to choose any way He wants to get into your heart and bless you.

—BRUCE WILKINSON, *Beyond Jabez*

Lord, please bless me any way you want, but please do it today.

WEDNESDAY

Rules of the Game

It is for freedom that Christ has set us free. Stand firm, then, and do not let yourselves be burdened again by a yoke of slavery.

GALATIANS 5:1

Many people don't understand the relationship between restriction and freedom.

You can't have freedom without proper restrictions. For example, could you have a football game if there were no sidelines and goal lines? Could you have a tennis match if there were no baselines? Could you have a baseball game if there were no foul lines? It would be chaos if players could go wherever they wanted to go. You only get to enjoy those games because there are guidelines that restrict the field of play.

God does not give us restrictions to be mean. God gives us rules to protect us from fouling out. He wants to prevent us from crossing the line so that the whistle has to be blown and we lose yardage in life.

—TONY EVANS, *God Can Not Be Trusted*

Lord, thank You for setting me free.

THURSDAY

Investing in Heaven

"Do not be afraid, little flock, for your Father has been pleased to give you the kingdom. Sell your possessions and give to the poor. Provide purses for yourselves that will not wear out, a treasure in heaven that will not be exhausted, where no thief comes near and no moth destroys. For where your treasure is, there your heart will be also."

Luke 12:32–34

Giving leads to freedom and a great sense of well-being. Why? Jesus said it is more blessed to give than to receive. These days we have it backwards. We think that it's all about receiving. But when you give, what you receive in return is a peace and a joy *right here and now*. You know that your giving is going to make a difference in eternity. You know that you are investing in treasures in heaven.

And when you live with a perspective like that—that your giving is going to bring this glorious blessing for the long haul—then you experience the short-term blessing of knowing that you're doing what God has called you to do. To be a giver, as He is a giver.

—Randy Alcorn, *The Treasure Principle*

Lord, help me to let go of things and see Your joy right now.

FRIDAY

Seeking Him First

Jesus replied: "'Love the Lord your God with all your heart and with all your soul and with all your mind.' This is the first and greatest commandment. And the second is like it: 'Love your neighbor as yourself.'"

Matthew 22:37–39

The first quality a person must have if they want to have an impact on any other person is a sincere, true, and deep love of Jesus Christ. Loving God with all your heart, mind, and soul and loving your neighbor are connected. When we seek after Him first, that's when He sends His Spirit into us and teaches us how to love on others.

Seek God first and He'll teach you and work through you to impact the people He brings across your path. It's about how we, as the body of Christ, live and interact with the world that is around us. To affect any person in the name of Christ means that we must first seek Him and look towards Christ, learning how He lived and what He did and how He interacts with men and women.

—Mike Yankoski, *Under the Overpass*

Lord, help me to see You first before doing any ministry.

WEEKEND

Outside Your Comfort Zone

The weapons we fight with are not the weapons of the world. On the contrary, they have divine power to demolish strongholds. We demolish arguments and every pretension that sets itself up against the knowledge of God, and we take captive every thought to make it obedient to Christ. And we will be ready to punish every act of disobedience, once your obedience is complete.

2 Corinthians 10:4–6

I have a deep desire to encourage every believer to journey further with God in both knowing and experiencing God and the Holy Spirit's power and presence in your life.

Don't stop in a comfort zone. Don't try to find a place where you feel you're secure. God will always move you out of your comfort zone so you can experience more of Him. If you try to settle down where you are, that's all you'll know of God. God always gives us a larger assignment, beyond our gifts, so that we can experience more of Him than we've ever known before.

Pursue the greater assignments God gives you.

—Henry and Mel Blackaby, *What's So Spiritual About Your Gifts?*

Lord, help me to not settle for comfort; stretch my faith.

MONDAY

SOCIAL-HOUR CHRISTIANS

For this reason, since the day we heard about you, we have not stopped praying for you and asking God to fill you with the knowledge of his will through all spiritual wisdom and understanding.

COLOSSIANS 1:9

Why do you go to church? Why do you get up on a Sunday morning and get dressed and drive someplace to attend a church service? Are you going for the meat and potatoes of Christianity, or because your friends are there and you'll have lunch together afterwards?

I encourage you to start being followers of the true, living God, not just social-hour Christians.

—RYAN DOBSON, *2 Live 4*

Lord, help me to view church as Your body, not just a gathering of people.

TUESDAY

Power in Clay Pots

But we have this treasure in jars of clay to show that this all-surpassing power is from God and not from us. We are hard pressed on every side, but not crushed; perplexed, but not in despair; persecuted, but not abandoned; struck down, but not destroyed. We always carry around in our body the death of Jesus, so that the life of Jesus may also be revealed in our body.

2 Corinthians 4:7–10

It's through our suffering and our trials and our wounds that God's glory is often revealed. We mustn't forget the eternal perspective in relation to our suffering.

"We have this treasure in jars of clay to show that this all-surpassing power is from God and not from us." Yes, we're unadorned clay pots, earthenware jars with chips and dings and flaws, and we're people with troubles and perplexities and weaknesses and fears. That's all we are without God. But with God, oh, we are so much more.

—Dr. Steve Stephens & Pam Vredevelt, *The Wounded Woman*

Lord, help me to remember the eternal perspective that You can use trials to mold me into Your image.

WEDNESDAY

The Disease of Covetousness

"You shall not covet your neighbor's house. You shall not covet your neighbor's wife, or his manservant or maidservant, his ox or donkey, or anything that belongs to your neighbor."

Exodus 20:17

It's incredible as children the things we feel we need to be happy. Then, of course, we grow up and the toys are bigger and more expensive, and it's a little hard to be content.

That's when the Lord reminds us that covetousness is something birthed within us. Until we realize that God is our provider, there's no way we can be free from the very unfortunate disease of seeking things rather than trusting God.

—Ron Mehl, *Right with God*

Lord, help me not to envy or be jealous of others; help me not to covet things or relationships; remind me that You are enough.

THURSDAY

Away from Temptation

No temptation has seized you except what is common to man. And God is faithful; he will not let you be tempted beyond what you can bear. But when you are tempted, he will also provide a way out so that you can stand up under it.

1 Corinthians 10:13

So many times we think, *If I only can be strong in this temptation....* And yet Jesus said, in training His disciples how to pray, "Lord, lead us not into temptation."

That's one of those secrets about praying that the prayer of Jabez reveals. *"Oh, God, keep me from evil."* Do you realize that God loves to answer that prayer? Not to make you strong in temptation, but to direct you away from it? To steer your eyes, your hands, and your feet away from where He knows evil is lurking?

Don't be a fool. Ask God to lead you away from that which He knows will tempt you.

—Bruce Wilkinson, *Beyond Jabez*

Lord, keep me from temptations I can't handle,
and teach me to trust that You'll protect me from evil.

FRIDAY

Unending Worship

Then I heard every creature in heaven and on earth and under the earth and on the sea, and all that is in them, singing: "To him who sits on the throne and to the Lamb be praise and honor and glory and power, for ever and ever!" The four living creatures said, "Amen," and the elders fell down and worshiped.

REVELATIONS 5:13–15

In the presence of God, right now, in this very instant, in this second, worship is going on. When we slip into deception and think that the world is only what we see in our little reality, then we miss out on the ultimate reality. What is it? Worship.

At some point, you're going to get settled in between the sheets tonight, and finally your eyes are going to close because you are running on a limited amount of resources. You're going to drop off into happy land, and when you do, worship is going to continue in the presence of God. It's going to continue all night long. And it's going to be that way forever, just like it has always been.

—LOUIE GIGLIO, *The Air I Breathe*

Lord, help me to wake up every morning ready to worship You.

WEEKEND

Overly Inward

Therefore, my dear friends, as you have always obeyed—
not only in my presence, but now much more in my absence—continue to work
out your salvation with fear and trembling, for it is God
who works in you to will and to act according to his good purpose.

PHILIPPIANS 2:12–13

The evangelical orientation is inward and subjective. We are far better at looking inward than we are at looking outward. Our sinful tendency is to direct and locate our faith in our emotional state or in our feelings at a given moment, even this very moment.

How often have you said to yourself when reading the Scriptures or listening to a sermon, "What do I feel about this?"

Instead, we need to extend our energies admiring, exploring, expositing, and extolling Jesus Christ.

—C. J. MAHANEY, *Living the Cross-Centered Life*

Lord, help me not to become absorbed
in myself but to meet others' needs.

MONDAY

Angel Ire

Just as there were many who were appalled at him—
his appearance was so disfigured beyond that of any man
and his form marred beyond human likeness—
so will he sprinkle many nations, and kings will shut their mouths
because of him. For what they were not told, they will see,
and what they have not heard, they will understand.

Isaiah 52:14–15

Hundreds of years before that day in Jerusalem when the Messiah was beaten and scourged, Isaiah recorded in Scripture how His face would be so disfigured that He would hardly be recognizable.

Can you imagine how God must have had to restrain all of heaven? The entire angelic host would doubtless have shouted, *This is our Lord. This is the King of kings. This is the Lord of heaven. You cannot let these men do this to Him!* The twelve legions of angels that Jesus spoke about in the Garden of Gethsemane must have been waiting on tiptoe to respond.

Yet the Father would have held them back and declared, *This is part of what I deliberately purposed from the beginning.*

—Henry Blackaby, *Experiencing the Cross*

Lord, thank You for sacrificing Your Son.

TUESDAY

On the Offensive

Wives, submit to your husbands as to the Lord....
Husbands, love your wives, just as Christ loved the church and gave himself up for her.... Children, obey your parents in the Lord.

EPHESIANS 5:22, 25; 6:1

In a culture that wants to destroy marriage and family, how do you and I go on the offensive? Here are some ideas.

First of all, realize that you, your marriage (if you're married), and your family, are living on a spiritual battlefield, not on a romantic balcony. Second, realize that your mate is never your enemy. Always know who your real enemy truly is. Third, stand firm and let God's Word be your guide when you don't know what to do. Fourth, pray without ceasing and give thanks in everything. God always meets the needs of the helpless sinner. Fifth, don't take temptations lightly. Flee immorality!

If you take these steps and others, you'll find that you can go on the offensive in a culture that wants to destroy your marriage and your family.

—DENNIS AND BARBARA RAINEY, *Growing a Spiritually Strong Family*

Lord, help me to defend the family and act to promote it.

WEDNESDAY

Restless Hearts

I thought in my heart, "Come now, I will test you with pleasure to find out what is good." But that also proved to be meaningless.... When I surveyed all that my hands had done and what I had toiled to achieve, everything was meaningless, a chasing after the wind; nothing was gained under the sun.

Ecclesiastes 2:1, 11

When we draw near to God in revival, something happens to us. We begin to see ourselves as we really are.

There came a time in my own life when I realized the utter emptiness of what I was doing. My pursuit of money and status was leading me to nothing but despair. In fact, the deeper into worldliness I went, the emptier I felt.

I would later learn the endearing truth of Augustine's words, that God created us for Himself and our hearts are restless until they find rest in Him.

—Pat Robertson, *Six Steps to Spiritual Revival*

Lord, help me to find rest in You.

THURSDAY

Providing Support

If anyone does not provide for his relatives, and especially for his immediate family, he has denied the faith and is worse than an unbeliever.

1 Timothy 5:8

Men's inclination to be a provider is not just a matter of wanting to. It's a burden and compulsion that goes very deep into the heart of a man. It also is their way of saying, "I love you." If the women in their lives don't realize that, they can make that burden worse.

For instance, a man comes home a little late and his wife says, "Honey, why did you work so late again? Don't you care about me and the kids?" And the husband is thinking, *Don't you realize that I'm working this hard because I love you and the kids?* It's his way of saying, "I love you."

Everyone works hard these days. But women need to do some work at recognizing how important the responsibility to provide is to men.

—Shaunti Feldhahn, *For Women Only*

Lord, help me to understand the drives toward provision and support.

FRIDAY

Power Team

But Moses said to God, "Who am I,
that I should go to Pharaoh and bring the Israelites out of Egypt?"
And God said, "I will be with you. And this will be the sign to you that
it is I who have sent you: When you have brought the people
out of Egypt, you will worship God on this mountain."

Exodus 3:11–12

When God chose Moses at the burning bush for a massive exodus mission, He found a guy on the back side of life in the middle of nowhere, who thought all of his best chances to make a difference with his life were gone. But when God found Moses, He said he had found His man, the one He was choosing to lead His people into the Promised Land.

A lot of people would have looked at Moses and said, "This guy, he doesn't have any of the qualifications to be the leader of a mission like this." But God knew it wasn't about Moses; it was all about Himself. God knows that He is the One who does all things well. That He is the One who holds all power, rule, and authority. And God, plus *anybody else*, is an overwhelmingly powerful team.

—Louie Giglio, *I Am Not But I Know I Am*

Lord, help me to believe that I can do all things through You.

WEEKEND

What Else Do I Need?

Psalm 73:23–26

I am always with you;
you hold me by my right hand.
You guide me with your counsel,
and afterward you will take me into glory.
Whom have I in heaven but you?
And earth has nothing I desire besides you.
My flesh and my heart may fail,
but God is the strength of my heart
and my portion forever.

Lord, you are my shepherd and my provider.
I am Yours, Lord!

MONDAY

Nothing Is Impossible

Jesus looked at them and said, "With man this is impossible, but with God all things are possible."

Matthew 19:26

I had already spoken to the king of Swaziland, announced it in parliament, spoken to the prime minister and various other leaders. In one week, Dream for Africa, with about a hundred volunteers, was going to plant ten thousand gardens for people who had no food, no money, and no hope of either.

On Monday, we planted three hundred gardens, and we were pretty tired. We changed the strategy, and Tuesday we planted six hundred gardens. We changed it again on Wednesday and planted twelve hundred gardens. On Thursday, I said, "Come back early because God needs to show us another way or we'll never reach our goal." On Friday morning we went out, and by the time that day was over, there was 12,874 gardens planted, and the whole country was cheering in celebration.

You see, when God's hand of power shows up, reality changes and everybody sees that God did it.

—Bruce Wilkinson, *Beyond Jabez*

Lord, help me to never underestimate Your power.

TUESDAY

Letter to God: Service

It was he who gave some...to prepare God's people for works of service, so that the body of Christ may be built up.

Ephesians 4:11–12

Dear God,

Help me to serve You right where You have placed me in life.

I want to love You with all that I am, to love the people You have put in my life, and to share my faith with others. I know my tendency to want to wait for the perfect place in time and life to do something grand for You. Forgive me for making excuses, for not living for You today. I know that life will never be perfect until I am at home in heaven with You.

And I know that it is in the imperfect world that Your love needs to be shared. So I am asking You to prune me and water me with Your Word so that I will grow into the woman You want me to be. Use me to sow seeds of faith in the lives of others, just as You used others to plant the same seeds in me.

Love,

Your princess, who wants to grow and help others grow too

—Sheri Rose Shepherd, *Prayers to My King*

WEDNESDAY

No Lone Rangers

Therefore each of you must put off falsehood and speak truthfully to his neighbor, for we are all members of one body.

Ephesians 4:25

If you try to be a lone ranger in your fight against sins such as lust, the truth is that very quickly you're going to be a dead ranger. Lust picks off stragglers. If you don't have support from other Christians, this is a sin that will only grow in strength and power.

Many times Christians say, "How could I ever talk about the area of sexual temptation with another believer? What would they think of me? I'll just handle it myself. In a couple years I'll share with a friend that I used to struggle with this."

Please don't do that. If you are isolated, lust is going to be able to rule you, to dominate you, and to destroy you. You need the help of other Christians.

—Joshua Harris, *Sex Is Not the Problem (Lust Is)*

Lord, help me to see that I am a member of Your body and I need fellow members to help me be victorious over my sin.

THURSDAY

Long-Term Thinking

Some of his disciples were remarking about how the temple was adorned with beautiful stones and with gifts dedicated to God. But Jesus said, "As for what you see here, the time will come when not one stone will be left on another; every one of them will be thrown down."

Luke 21:5–6

Excuse me, sir…I just got into town tonight and got no place to stay. There's a shelter around the corner, and they need seven dollars. I got a couple. I was wondering if you could spare a five."

"Listen, dude. If I took that five bucks and invested it, in thirty years it would be worth four or five times that. What do I get if I give it to you?"

A good investment counselor is going to tell you, "Don't think short-term. Don't think just thirty days ahead. Don't think just three years ahead. Think thirty years ahead."

Well, Jesus says, "You know what, thirty years ahead is really thinking short-term." Don't ask yourself, *How is this investment of my time and my money going to pay off in thirty years?* Ask, *How is it going to pay off in 30 million years? In eternity?*

—Randy Alcorn, *The Treasure Principle*

Lord, help me to develop a long-term perspective on all that I do.

FRIDAY

Wherever the Master Is

"The man who loves his life will lose it, while the man who hates his life in this world will keep it for eternal life. Whoever serves me must follow me; and where I am, my servant also will be. My Father will honor the one who serves me."

John 12:25–26

I believe God has placed in the heart of every one of His children the awareness that they need to know and do the will of God. They come to want to serve Him. But what's crucial, though? A relationship with the living Christ.

Jesus said in John 12 that if people want to serve Him, they need to be where Jesus is. "Wherever the Master is, there the servant must be also."

We do not determine how we serve God; the Master determines that. So we don't keep telling God what we want to do for Him. He says, "You're the servant and I'm the Master. I'll determine where you serve and how you serve and when you serve."

—Henry and Mel Blackaby, *What's So Spiritual About Your Gifts?*

Lord, help me to serve You today.

WEEKEND

Defeating Deception

To the Jews who had believed him, Jesus said,
"If you hold to my teaching, you are really my disciples.
Then you will know the truth, and the truth will set you free."

John 8:31–32

There's only one secret to defeating a lie, and that is to know and obey the truth.

Truth is that which conforms to reality. God is the ultimate reality; He is the source of truth. When you are acting on what God says in the Bible and walking in the truth, you automatically defeat the lie and rob it of its power. Why? Because the lie only has power when you're responding to it. It loses its zip when you say, "I'm not responding, even though I want to."

All of a sudden you'll discover that that lie, that deception, wasn't nearly as powerful as it purported itself to be.

—Tony Evans, *God Can Not Be Trusted*

Lord, help me to keep the truth in my heart.

MONDAY

More than a Rebate

And he took bread, gave thanks and broke it, and gave it to them, saying, "This is my body given for you; do this in remembrance of me." In the same way, after the supper he took the cup, saying, "This cup is the new covenant in my blood, which is poured out for you."

LUKE 22:19–20

The word *redemption* doesn't mean much in our society. Maybe it might mean you get a nickel back for your aluminum can. It might mean you send something in that you purchased in order to get a twenty-dollar rebate on a computer. But in the Bible, redemption is full of meaning. For Christ, what redemption meant is that He is purchasing something back to the Father that had been lost. The focus of His redemption is us. To purchase us back to the Father, He needed to pay the penalty for our sin. With the incredible love of God and the incredible holiness of God, meeting on one day at one time in the person of Christ, God was able to pour His wrath out on the Son and pour His love out on us.

—RICK MCKINLEY, *Jesus in the Margins*

Lord, thank You for redeeming me.

TUESDAY

Asking Isn't Selfish

Answer me, O Lord, out of the goodness of your love;
in your great mercy turn to me.
Do not hide your face from your servant;
answer me quickly, for I am in trouble.

Psalm 69:16–17

My friend and I were having lunch. Both of us had eyed the cheesecake during the meal, and there was only one piece left. My friend got up to answer the telephone. I thought to myself, *You know, he can't possibly love cheesecake as much as I do. And besides, he's a forgiving friend.* Before I realized it, I had eaten the whole piece.

What would that be called? Well, that would be called selfishness. But what if there were two pieces of cheesecake and both of us asked for a piece? Would that be selfishness? No.

What would have happened if my friend had said, "I don't like cheesecake. Please have the piece." That wouldn't be selfishness either.

In fact, when you ask God for a blessing, who's losing a piece? The answer is no one. Asking God for a blessing cannot be selfish.

—Bruce Wilkinson, *Beyond Jabez*

Lord, help me to understand Your willingness to bless me.

WEDNESDAY

Never Fickle

And [God] passed in front of Moses, proclaiming, "The Lord, the Lord, the compassionate and gracious God, slow to anger, abounding in love and faithfulness, maintaining love to thousands, and forgiving wickedness, rebellion and sin. Yet he does not leave the guilty unpunished."

Exodus 34:6–7

We might imagine that God becomes disgusted with our meandering disobedience and decides to stand us up. "I'll teach them a lesson!" we picture Him saying.

Perhaps we're afraid that if we don't somehow keep ourselves in God's spotlight, He'll get too busy juggling galaxies and fulfilling prophecy. Or worse yet, we might so exasperate Him that He won't take the time to sort out the complicated mess we've gotten ourselves into.

But your God is never fickle. He'll never give up on you. H never become distracted. His interest will never cool with passin years. You don't have to worry about trying to impress Him. In His constant desire is to draw you closer into His embrace.

—Joni Eareckson Tada, *31 Days to Intimacy with God*

Lord, thank You for Your faithfulness.

THURSDAY

Unsearchable Things

"This is what the Lord says, he who made the earth, the Lord who formed it and established it—the Lord is his name: 'Call to me and I will answer you and tell you great and unsearchable things you do not know.'"

Jeremiah 33:2–3

The danger and the deception of sin is that it causes us to think somehow that God is on our level. He is not. He is great and eternal. God spoke and the whole universe came into being. His ways, His wisdom, His insight, e unsearchable and unknowable to us.

Our lives work best when we remember that God is greater ur greatest thought of Him, our greatest imagination And at the end of the day, in this life, none of us can just how big He is. But we do know that He loves ow that He cares for us. And we know that He is d organizing and orchestrating all the events of nd for our good.

e Giglio, *I Am Not But I Know I Am*

reaching out to us out of Your greatness.

FRIDAY

Born with a Song

Sing to the Lord a new song,
for he has done marvelous things;
his right hand and his holy arm
have worked salvation for him.
The Lord has made his salvation known
and revealed his righteousness to the nations.

Psalm 98:1–2

I like to say that each of us a song that's born in us. You may be thinking, *Chris, I'm the most unmusical person ever. I'm tone deaf. I can't clap on two and four. I don't know anything about notes. I don't know anything about scales. I don't know how to write a song.*

But the song I'm talking about is the way God has uniquely gifted you. God has given you something unique. He has knit you specifically for His purposes.

I pray that you could long for that song God has placed in you, the way God has wired you that He hasn't wired anybody else.

—Chris Tomlin, *The Way I Was Made*

Lord, help me sing the song You place in my life.

WEEKEND

Letter to God: Trust

And we know that in all things God works for the good of those who love him, who have been called according to his purpose.

Romans 8:28

Dear God,

Sometimes I'm so discouraged by the way situations work out, by the way my plans for my life fail. My hopes and dreams dissolve into disappointment, and I find myself feeling hopeless. When I'm at that place, help me to trust You more.

Help me to know that You're working on my behalf, even when I don't see things happening the way I want them to. Give me the strength to do the right thing, to keep obeying and trusting You, even when everything seems to be going wrong. I ask You to renew my hope and open my eyes to the spiritual significance of life's disappointments, challenges, and frustrations. I am choosing to believe that You, my Father, know what is best for me and that You are in control of the tiniest details in my life.

Love,

Your princess, who wants Your will for her life

—Sheri Rose Shepherd, *Prayers to My King*

MONDAY

Outward Expression

She makes coverings for her bed;
she is clothed in fine linen and purple.
Her husband is respected at the city gate,
where he takes his seat among the elders of the land....
Charm is deceptive, and beauty is fleeting;
but a woman who fears the LORD is to be praised.
Give her the reward she has earned,
and let her works bring her praise at the city gate.

PROVERBS 31:22–23, 30–31

We all know that it's what's on the inside that counts. But maybe we've also tended to move from that idea to believing that what's on the outside doesn't matter. The truth is, it does matter to husbands to see their wives be willing to make an effort for them.

Just as women want men to love them in the way they need to be loved, the area of physical appearance is one in which women can love their men in the way they need to be loved.

—SHAUNTI FELDHAHN, *For Women Only*

Lord, help me to be attractive inside and out.

TUESDAY

Worth It All

"Again, the kingdom of heaven is like a merchant looking for fine pearls.
When he found one of great value,
he went away and sold everything he had and bought it."

MATTHEW 13:45

The value we place on something will determine the degree of passion we show for it. It's the principle that Jesus was trying to teach us in the Parable of the Pearl.

The kingdom of God is about your past being forgiven, your destiny being secure, and your life gaining purpose and meaning. But if we're not careful, the distractions of life can rob our time and keep us blind to the blessings of the kingdom.

The kingdom will cost you everything, but it's worth it all—and more.

—STUART BRISCOE, *Time Bandits*

Lord, help me to seek things in life that last.

WEDNESDAY

Clear Conscience

And no wonder, for Satan himself masquerades as an angel of light. It is not surprising, then, if his servants masquerade as servants of righteousness. Their end will be what their actions deserve.

2 Corinthians 11:14–15

Can you tell the difference between the accusations of the devil and the conviction of the Holy Spirit? If not, you may be continually confessing sins that God has already forgiven.

Satan plagues us with false guilt because he wants to break our fellowship with the Father. If you have confessed your sins and honestly confronted God regarding them, the way you take care of guilt is to say, *Be gone, Satan, for it is written who shall lay anything to the charge of God's elect? It is God who justifies.*

I want you to know today that it is God's will that you have a clear conscience.

—Erwin Lutzer, *After You've Blown It*

Lord, may I rest in Your forgiveness.

THURSDAY

"Send Someone Who Needs God"

The Spirit told Philip, "Go to that chariot and stay near it." Then Peter ran up to the chariot and he heard the man reading Isaiah the prophet. "Do you understand what you are reading?" Philip asked. "How can I," he said, "unless someone explains it to me?"

Acts 8:29–31

I don't think he was nineteen yet. He came bursting into the room and said, "It worked! I prayed that prayer. You know, that Jabez prayer, and it worked." I asked him what happened.

"I was walking down a road and I asked God, 'Would You please bless me? Would You expand my territory? Would You send somebody right now who needs You?'" Then he said, "I turned around, and the next car driving along this old, dirt road stopped." He said he got in and said to the young man who was driving. "I'm here to share about God. Are you interested?" And the man said, "I just prayed and said to God, 'If You're real, send somebody to me.'"

You know, my friend, maybe it's your turn to ask God to send you somebody who needs Him.

—Bruce Wilkinson, *Beyond Jabez*

Lord, help me to be sensitive and obedient to Your directions.

FRIDAY

What We Deserve

If we walk in the light, as he is in the light, we have fellowship with one another, and the blood of Jesus, his Son, purifies us from all sin. If we claim to be without sin, we deceive ourselves and the truth is not in us. If we confess our sins, he is faithful and just and will forgive us our sins and purify us from all unrighteousness.

1 John 1:7–9

If you want to be a grace-giver, you need first to realize that you constantly need grace yourself. Every day you receive an amazing gift of grace from God. Every day we receive His longsuffering and patience.

Maybe your boss is mean and unfair. When he treats you like dirt, you might be tempted to wish that he "gets what he deserves." But is he so different from you?

None of us want to get what we "deserve" in life. When we begin to realize the grace we have received, we will be able to have grace to give to others.

—Richard Blackaby, *Putting a Face on Grace*

Lord, help me to be patient with everyone, because I am fallen too.

WEEKEND

The Preacher

How, then, can they call on the one they have not believed in? And how can they believe in the one of whom they have not heard? And how can they hear without someone preaching to them?

Romans 10:14

When you hear the word *preacher*, what do you think of? Is it a guy standing behind a pulpit wearing a suit and tie who runs the church?

Actually, no single image comes to my mind, because I believe we were all called to preach. Everyone was called to preach the Word of Jesus Christ in whatever way possible. You can be a mechanic and a preacher. You can be a doctor and be a preacher. You can be a lawyer and be a preacher. I took fourteen high school skateboarders down to Ecuador. They were all preachers. They just happened to ride a skateboard.

In what ways is God opening doors for you to spread the gospel? Is it to your neighbor? Is it to the local basketball team you coach? Is it to your family? We all need to look for ways in which we can spread the Word of Jesus Christ.

—Ryan Dobson, *2 Live 4*

Lord, help me to be ready to preach the gospel at any time.

MONDAY

The Branch Will Bear Fruit

Isaiah 11:1–5

A shoot will come up from the stump of Jesse;
from his roots a Branch will bear fruit.
The Spirit of the Lord will rest on him—
the Spirit of wisdom and of understanding,
the Spirit of counsel and of power,
the Spirit of knowledge and of the fear of the Lord—
and he will delight in the fear of the Lord.
He will not judge by what he sees with his eyes,
or decide by what he hears with his ears;
but with righteousness he will judge the needy,
with justice he will give decisions for the poor of the earth.
He will strike the earth with the rod of his mouth;
with the breath of his lips he will slay the wicked.
Righteousness will be his belt
and faithfulness the sash around his waist.

Lord, thank You for Your mighty Spirit.

TUESDAY

Forever the Same

Moses said to God, "Suppose I go to the Israelites and say to them, 'The God of your fathers has sent me to you,' and they ask me, 'What is his name?' Then what shall I tell them?" God said to Moses, "I am who I am. This is what you are to say to the Israelites: 'I AM has sent me to you.'"

EXODUS 3:13–14

Imagine yourself face-to-face with the glory of God, as Moses was when he encountered Him in the burning bush on the back side of Mt. Sinai. Trembling in fear, he asked God, "What is Your name?" And the answer comes back, "My name is *I Am that I Am*. Tell them that *I Am* has sent you to them."

What kind of a name is *I Am*? It's translated from the Hebrew word *hayah*, the verb "to be," meaning that God is always ever present and the same. He has never had a beginning. He is never going to have an end. He is always the same God in every moment in every situation to every person. He is *I Am that I Am*.

—LOUIE GIGLIO, *I Am Not But I Know I Am*

Lord, thank You that You are the same yesterday, today, and tomorrow.

WEDNESDAY

True Family Values

This is a profound mystery—but I am talking about Christ and the church. However, each one of you also must love his wife as he loves himself, and the wife must respect her husband.

Ephesians 5:32–33

There's a lot of talk today about family values. It's too bad that many people never get around to living for family values.

One of the most important things we did early on in our marriage was that we sat down and came up with a list of our top ten values. We prioritized that list, and then we set a course for our marriage and family that continues on to this day. We have sought to make decisions according to those convictions we value.

Want to know what our top three were? Number one, teach our children to fear God. Number two, teach our children to love God. And number three, to be involved in the great commission.

What are your family's values?

—Dennis and Barbara Rainey, *Growing a Spiritually Strong Family*

Lord, help me to build up my family.

THURSDAY

Home Base

Like a bird that strays from its nest
is a man who strays from his home.

Proverbs 27:8

Home is the most important place for a man to be affirmed. If a married man knows that his wife believes in him, he's empowered to do better in every area of his life. Men tend to think of life as a competition and a battle. They can go duke it out only if they can come home to someone who supports them unconditionally, who will wipe their brow and tell them they can do it.

One of our close friends told me, "It's all about whether my wife thinks I can. A husband can slay dragons, climb mountains, and win great victories if he believes that his wife believes he can."

The most important place for men to be affirmed is at home. This does not tear women down; it helps build men up.

—Sh'aunti Feldhahn, *For Women Only*

Lord, thank You for the chance to accomplish
Your plan in my life through strong relationships.

FRIDAY

Great Is Your Reward

"Blessed are you when people insult you, persecute you and falsely say all kinds of evil against you because of me. Rejoice and be glad, because great is your reward in heaven, for in the same way they persecuted the prophets who were before you."

Matthew 5:11–12

You've heard how Christians in New Testament times were fed to lions for entertainment. Have you ever wondered how they could walk into that coliseum—singing?

The secret is that they believed something Jesus said. They believed it so thoroughly that it changed their lives.

Jesus said that if people revile and persecute you and lie about you because of Him, then be glad. Glad for what? Well, listen to the rest of the verse. Jesus said, "Great is your reward in heaven."

In other words, Jesus said, "You suffer here for Me—wait till you see how I reward you in heaven. And the reward isn't small or medium. It's great. That's why you should rejoice."

—Bruce Wilkinson, *A Life God Rewards*

Lord, help me to see that no challenges of today can trump the joy of eternity.

WEEKEND

Drive-Through Prayer

"And when you pray, do not keep on babbling like pagans, for they think they will be heard because of their many words."

Matthew 6:7

We typically say our prayers as casually as we order a burger at the drive-through. "I'll have one solved problem and two blessings. Leave off the hassles, please."

Here we are before the King of kings. Dare we limit our discussion? Jesus tells us to begin like this. "When you pray, say, 'Father, hallowed be your name, your kingdom come.'" This is no feeble request. It's a bold appeal for God to occupy every corner of your life.

Who are you to ask such a thing? Well, you're His child, for heaven's sake. The Bible invites us to come boldly to the very throne of God. You can respond to the invitation of God to request His kingdom because you are a child of the King.

—Max Lucado, *Turn*

Lord, help me to pray reverently but boldly.

MONDAY

The Foundation of Forgiveness

Blessed is he whose transgressions are forgiven, whose sins are covered....
When I kept silent, my bones wasted away through my groaning all day long....
Then I acknowledged my sin to you and did not cover up my iniquity.
I said, "I will confess my transgressions to the LORD" —
and you forgave the guilt of my sin.

PSALM 32:1, 3, 5

When it comes to the sin of lust, it's so important to remember that we can only change when we understand the truth of the forgiveness that God has made available through Jesus Christ, through His sacrifice in our place.

My friend taught me to pray from Psalm 32. I love to insert my name in there. "Blessed is Joshua, whose sin the Lord does not count against him." If you're a person who is struggling with temptation in the area of lust, you need to base your fight on the forgiveness that God has already made available. That has to be the foundation.

—JOSHUA HARRIS, *Sex Is Not the Problem (Lust Is)*

Lord, help me to realize that my foundation is in Your salvation.

TUESDAY

The Essence of Idolatry

"You will not surely die," the serpent said to the woman. "For God knows that when you eat of it your eyes will be opened, and you will be like God, knowing good and evil."

Genesis 3:4–5

One way the devil seeks to deceive us is by telling us that we can be like God. To make more of yourself than you ought to is the essence of idolatry.

It's a little like you're a rebellious, arrogant, self-centered teenager in the house, who wants independence, who wants to act like an adult, but who doesn't have the capacity to handle it. Well, you and I are in God's house. As soon as *you* can start creating your own world and running your own universe, *then* you can make the claim to be like God. But in His house, there is only one parent.

So we've got to stop acting as if we're going to grow up and be like God. There is only One God.

—Tony Evans, *God Can Not Be Trusted*

Lord, help me not to listen to the devil's lies.

WEDNESDAY

As We Are

When I consider your heavens, the work of your fingers,
the moon and the stars, which you have set in place,
what is man that you are mindful of him,
the son of man that you care for him?

Psalm 8:3–4

I often remind people that they are just one of 6.4 billion people floating today on this planet called Earth, which is orbiting around the ordinary sun and the Milky Way galaxy of hundreds of millions of stars, which is just one of hundreds of billions of galaxies out there in the known universe that we can see. Often people respond with, "Wow! When you say that, it makes me feel small." I always reply, "I'm not trying to make you feel small; I'm trying to help you *know* that you are small."

Humility is looking up to see that God is the Creator of all things. And just a glimpse of Him resizes us in an instant. I think pride is seeing ourselves as we're not. Humility is constantly gazing into the eyes of God and seeing Him as He is.

—Louie Giglio, *I Am Not But I Know I Am*

Lord, thank You for being mindful of us.

THURSDAY

Healing the Land

So whether you eat or drink or whatever you do,
do it all for the glory of God.

1 Corinthians 10:31

What if we applied the filter of 1 Corinthians 10:31 to our government? Do it all for the glory of God? Manage budgets to the glory of God? Determine Homeland Security for the glory of God? Elect officials to the glory of God, not for the glory of Democrats or Republicans or Independents, but all for the glory of God?

He said if My people who are called by My name are sorry for what they have done, if they pray and obey Me and stop their evil ways, I will hear from heaven. I will forgive their sin, and I will heal their land.

—Max Lucado, *Turn*

Lord, help me to view what I do at work
from the standard of Your glory.

FRIDAY

This Is Not Our Home

But you are a chosen people, a royal priesthood, a holy nation, a people belonging to God, that you may declare the praises of him who called you out of darkness into his wonderful light.

1 Peter 2:9

I'm really convinced that the greatest deterrent to giving is the illusion that this earth is our home.

Suppose your home is in France and you're visiting America for three months, living in a hotel. And then you're told, "Well, you can't bring anything back to France on your flight home, but while you're here, you can earn money, and then you can mail deposits back to your bank in France."

Would you fill your hotel room with expensive furniture and wall hangings? Of course not. You'd send your money back to where your home is, where it will be yours for the long term, not just for the short term.

The Bible tells us that we are pilgrims. We're aliens. We're ambassadors away from our true country, representing it to the world. Heaven, not earth, is our true home.

—Randy Alcorn, *The Treasure Principle*

Lord, help me to view this earth as my temporary home.

WEEKEND

A Little Child Shall Lead Them

"But wisdom is proved right by all her children."

Luke 7:35

In 2003, college students Mike Yankoski and Sam Purvis spent more than five months living on the streets of America to learn what it means to be homeless.

When we were homeless in Washington DC, we went to panhandle one evening near the Potomac River. For about three hours we panhandled and only made $1.18. Just as we were getting frustrated and going to pack up, this group of about twelve kids came walking across the boardwalk toward us. The smallest one looked down and said, "You don't have any money at all, do you?" He pulled out $1.25 and sat it down in the guitar case.

In that moment, the child had seen our need and, because he hadn't learned yet how to pretend that people don't exist, he showed mercy to us.

—Mike Yankoski, *Under the Overpass*

Lord, help me to see others as if through the eyes of a child.

MONDAY

Thy Will Be Done

He went away a second time and prayed, "My Father, if it is not possible for this cup to be taken away unless I drink it, may your will be done...." [He] prayed the third time, saying the same thing. Then he returned to the disciples and said to them, "...Look, the hour is near, and the Son of Man is betrayed into the hands of sinners. Rise, let us go! Here comes my betrayer!"

MATTHEW 26:42–46

In the earthly ministry of God's Son, the time for teaching and the time for the working of miracles had come to an end. What remained of the Savior's work was that which was the most necessary and the most difficult: the Cross.

This is what confronted Jesus when He went to His Father in prayer in Gethsemane. He pleaded, "Abba, Father, all things are possible for You. Take this cup away from Me." But the Father had to answer, *I can't. I can't take it away. My eternal purpose was for this very moment.*

And at that point, everything in the Father's eternal purpose for humanity's redemption depended on whether the Savior would say, "Not My will, but Thine be done."

—HENRY BLACKABY, *Experiencing the Cross*

Lord, thank You for doing the Father's will.

TUESDAY

THE RISK OF FAITH

Then Peter got down out of the boat, walked on the water and came toward Jesus. But when he saw the wind, he was afraid and, beginning to sink, cried out, "Lord, save me!" Immediately Jesus reached out his hand and caught him. "You of little faith," he said, "why did you doubt?"

MATTHEW 14:29–31

Perhaps down deep in your heart you wish that you could something more for God, beyond what you're able even to think of. Do you know what that would require of you?

It would require from you not only a greater obedience to God, but a greater faith in God—a risk of faith. What is it about God that you don't trust enough to step out? Do you actually believe that He's going to supply all your needs? Do you actually believe He has all power and will intervene for you when you need it? Do you actually believe that what He says is true, that you can do all things through Him?

On that basis, go ahead and step out of the boat, and begin to walk on the water.

—BRUCE WILKINSON, *Beyond Jabez*

Lord, help me to keep my eyes on You
and not on the signs of the storm around me.

WEDNESDAY

Anxious for Nothing

"For I know the plans I have for you," declares the Lord, *"plans to prosper you and not to harm you, plans to give you hope and a future."*

Jeremiah 29:11

If you're someone who is dealing with anxiety and uncertainty about your future, I have some very encouraging words for you. You are normal. Welcome to the world. Welcome to reality.

All of us deal with it. All of us deal with worry and apprehension about the future. And I just say, from the experience of my own life, that God will move mountains to put you where He wants you.

He doesn't play hide-and-seek. You will look back and go, "Wow, I had no idea how God was using all these things in my life to put me right here." Take hope!

—Chris Tomlin, *The Way I Was Made*

Lord, help me not to be anxious and to rest in You.

THURSDAY

Trusting like Children

"See that you do not look down on one of these little ones. For I tell you that their angels in heaven always see the face of my Father in heaven."

MATTHEW 18:10–11

Jesus said that unless we become like little children, we cannot enter the kingdom of God.

Kids don't hold a lot of weight in our society. They're cute. We love them. But at the same time, we don't really go to them to say, "Can you show us the way to the kingdom of God?" And yet Christ comes on the scene and He elevates these little kids and He says, "You know what? Unless you guys are willing to follow them, you're not going to make it."

Little kids have an innate sense of trust, a trust that in a cruel world can get them in trouble. But in the kingdom of heaven, Jesus says, "That is the mark of ownership in My kingdom. Be willing to engage life like that little child, because that freedom is what life is like in My kingdom."

—RICK MCKINLEY, *Jesus in the Margins*

Lord, help me to seek You as a child.

FRIDAY

Letter to God: Regret

Godly sorrow brings repentance that leads to salvation and leaves no regret, but worldly sorrow brings death.

2 Corinthians 7:10

Dear God,

Sometimes I look back on my life and I regret the days I wasted by not living for You. I let so many circumstances interfere with our love relationship. I let people and pain keep me paralyzed, unable to live as Your princess.

I'm so grateful that You can take whatever I give You now and whatever time I have left here on earth and use it for Your kingdom. I'm glad You can use me to finish the work You set out for me to do from the beginning of time. And I praise You for being able to redeem the days that were lost, Lord.

Help me let go of what's wrong and cling to the future of hope in You and a heart filled with the joy of my salvation.

Love,

Your princess, who finds hope in You

—Sheri Rose Shepherd, *Prayers to My King*

WEEKEND

Wind-in-Your-Face Christianity

Am I now trying to win the approval of men, or of God? Or am I trying to please men?

Galatians 1:10

I went to a hot rod motorcycle show recently. My friends and I were hanging out and having a great time. Then we noticed some guys. They didn't ride up on their bikes. They drove up in a truck, with a trailer on the back. On the trailer was a motorcycle. When they arrived, they wheeled the bike down into a parking spot and wiped it down and stood there, as if to say, *Look what a great bike I've got.*

We call them trailer queens. I think there are some trailer-queen Christians out there too. I mean people holding their Christianity like a possession. I want you to experience wind-in-your-face Christianity. Not the trailer-queen kind.

—Ryan Dobson, *2 Live 4*

Lord, help me not to care about the approval of others.

MONDAY

A Little Child Will Lead Them

Isaiah 11:6–9

The wolf will live with the lamb,
the leopard will lie down with the goat,
the calf and the lion and the yearling together;
and a little child will lead them.
The cow will feed with the bear,
their young will lie down together,
and the lion will eat straw like the ox.
The infant will play near the hole of the cobra,
and the young child put his hand into the viper's nest.
They will neither harm nor destroy
on all my holy mountain,
for the earth will be full of the knowledge of the Lord
as the waters cover the sea.

Lord, thank You for a future full of peace and hope.

TUESDAY

Sponges and Turtles

When I kept silent,
my bones wasted away
through my groaning all day long.
For day and night
your hand was heavy upon me;
my strength was sapped
as in the heat of summer

Psalm 32:3–4

There are two types of people in this world. Sponges and turtles. Turtles are the sorts of people whose stress and anxiety just roll off their back. Then there are sponges. They just seem to soak up life's stress and anxiety.

How do you become a turtle if you think you're a sponge? It might be genetics, but oftentimes it has to do with the amount of trauma you experienced early in your life. Nevertheless, you make everything worse when you keep things locked up inside and don't talk to anybody.

—Dr. Steve Stephens & Pam Vredevelt, *The Wounded Woman*

Lord, help me to be honest with myself
and talk to You about everything.

WEDNESDAY

Self-Controlled Lives

Clothe yourselves with the Lord Jesus Christ,
and do not think about how to gratify the desires of the sinful nature.

Romans 13:14

God has given us something so wonderful in the intimacy and passion that is to be reserved for marriage, and yet our lust wants to destroy that. I think one of the most important things we can realize is that lust is a real problem.

Lust wants to ruin our souls. Lust wants to steal from us the good things that God has in store for us. It's a lie to believe that lust is no big deal. It's also a lie to think that this is just the way it is; we can't control our desires.

God has provided for us in His Word and through His Holy Spirit what we need to live self-controlled lives, to use our sexuality in a way that is pleasing to Him. And with His grace, we can do that.

—Joshua Harris, *Sex Is Not the Problem (Lust Is)*

Lord, help me to draw on Your wonderful grace
so that I can please You with my body.

THURSDAY

The Hindrance of Unbelief

See to it, brothers, that none of you has a sinful, unbelieving heart that turns away from the living God. But encourage one another daily, as long as it is called Today, so that none of you may be hardened by sin's deceitfulness.

HEBREWS 3:12–13

Why you do not see the hand of God in your life on a regular basis?

I once spent two days with fifty-six major international Christian leaders, and I asked them that same question. *Why in your organizations are you not seeing the power of God intervene?* The number one reason they gave was unbelief. I asked them what they meant. They put it this way: "We don't really believe that God is going to break through, that He wants to break through, or that He can break through."

If you go back to the time when Jesus walked upon this earth, the Scripture says that when He didn't do great and mighty works in their midst it was because of unbelief. Could that be that the same hindrance in your life today?

—BRUCE WILKINSON, *Beyond Jabez*

Lord, help me to encourage my brothers and sisters on to a stronger belief in You.

FRIDAY

God of Second Chances

He has shown us kindness in the sight of the kings of Persia:
He has granted us new life to rebuild the house of our God and repair its ruins,
and he has given us a wall of protection in Judah and Jerusalem.

Ezra 9:9

I remember when I was in my very first beauty pageant. They said, "Just smile at the judges." Well, I kept just walking and smiling, and I walked right off the end of the runway. I got back up on that runway, and in my ripped-up evening gown I looked at the judges, and said, "I just wanted you to remember me."

They did. I won. The Bible says a righteous man can fall seven times, but he will get back up again. And I think that about how even if we think that we didn't come from the right family, or we've made all these mistakes, or we've been hurt or cursed by someone, even then God can use us.

Good news: God is the God of second chances.

—Sheri Rose Shepherd, *My Prince Will Come*

Lord, thank You for remembering me
and giving me a new life.

WEEKEND

Beyond Our Talents

Moses said to the Lord, "O Lord, I have never been eloquent, neither in the past nor since you have spoken to your servant. I am slow of speech and tongue." The Lord said to him, "Who gave man his mouth? Who makes him deaf or mute? Who gives him sight or makes him blind? Is it not I, the Lord? Now go; I will help you speak and will teach you what to say." But Moses said, "O Lord, please send someone else to do it."

Exodus 4:10–13

One of the dangers of trying to discover our spiritual gifts, which often are just our talents and abilities, is that we don't then follow God's assignment.

For instance, if God were to give us an assignment that we thought was impossible for us, we might say, "But dear God, that's not where my spiritual gifts lie."

God says, "Obey Me." His goal is to let the world see not our talents, but how He works through ordinary people. And so He will often give us assignments that we cannot do because His goal is not to make us successful, but to reveal Himself. And only when we go beyond our talents and abilities to something that only God can do will the world come face-to-face with God.

—Henry and Mel Blackaby, *What's So Spiritual About Your Gifts?*

Lord, help me to be obedient when You call me.

MONDAY

Spiritual Nourishment

And do this, understanding the present time. The hour has come for you to wake up from your slumber, because our salvation is nearer now than when we first believed. The night is nearly over; the day is almost here. So let us put aside the deeds of darkness and put on the armor of light.

Romans 13:11–12

Did you know that good, strong spiritual growth is directly dependent upon nourishing your soul with good and spiritual nutrients?

Where do you start if you're going to grow spiritually? The Bible contains the true health food for our souls that we need for daily living. If you don't read the Scripture together as a couple or as a husband or a wife, you need to do so daily. Memorize Scripture. Read the Bible at mealtime. Use Scripture to draw your life from.

If you do, you'll grow a strong, spiritual marriage and family.

—Dennis and Barbara Rainey, *Growing a Spiritually Strong Family*

Lord, help me to seek spiritual nourishment every chance I get.

TUESDAY

Living Small

But who is able to build a temple for him, since the heavens, even the highest heavens, cannot contain him? Who then am I to build a temple for him, except as a place to burn sacrifices before him?

2 Chronicles 2:6

While culture and everything around us tell us that we've got to be big, maybe the most freeing thing we can do is to live small. And by living small, I mean to live our lives in such a way that they reflect the greatness of God.

In the story of God, we have lost the plot and put ourselves at the center. We start to demand our way, we're frustrated that things don't turn out the way we planned, and we forget that life is not about us. Life, at the end of the day, is the grand story of God, and our lives are all for Him. Living small today is living our lives in such a way that people around us see Him and glorify Him.

—Louie Giglio, *I Am Not But I Know I Am*

Lord, help me to live mindful of my smallness and Your greatness.

WEDNESDAY

A King's Heart

The king's heart is in the hand of the Lord;
he directs it like a watercourse wherever he pleases.

Proverbs 21:1

How do you respond when you don't trust the heart of a leadership?

The Scriptures tell us that the king's heart is like a stream of water directed by the Lord, and He turns it wherever He pleases. A king (or a president or prime minister) may think he calls the shots, but he doesn't. God holds sway over his throne. The stubborn will of the most powerful monarch on earth is directed by God as easily as a farmer reroutes a shallow canal into his farm.

Next time you're concerned or worried about the direction of a nation or a people, remember that God manages the hearts of all nations.

—Max Lucado, *Turn*

Lord, help me to pray for the world's leaders.

THURSDAY

Autonomy from God

But because of your stubbornness and your unrepentant heart,
you are storing up wrath against yourself for the day of God's wrath,
when his righteous judgment will be revealed.
God "will give to each person according to what he has done."

Romans 2:5–6

Once my brother was kicked out of our home because he demanded to be autonomous from our father. He soon discovered that with no job, no car, only the clothes on his back, and in the middle of winter, autonomy was not a good thing.

Well, the human race is discovering that autonomy is not a good thing. We may not acknowledge it because we've distanced ourselves from God. But we're finding marriages that cannot be sustained. Parent-child relationships that are strained. Lack of fulfillment in money and power and success. Crime, world conflict, emptiness. Autonomy from God isn't a good thing. Why? Because it always results in chaos.

Don't seek to be autonomous from God; stay in the family.

—Tony Evans, *God Can Not Be Trusted*

Lord, help me to resist the world's
influence toward self-sufficiency.

FRIDAY

Evidence of Life

Now that you have purified yourselves by obeying the truth so that you have sincere love for your brothers, love one another deeply, from the heart. For you have been born again, not of perishable seed, but of imperishable, through the living and enduring word of God.

1 Peter 1:22–23

If you're a parent, your child may have asked about when he or she was born. Children never seem to tire of the story, even when you tell them that the important thing is not how they were born, but *that* they were born. That they're here today, alive.

The evidence of being born is life. Likewise, the evidence of being born again is new life. But it's not just a one-time deal that we experience and forget about. It's about gradual, but discernable change that shows up in everything.

—Stuart Briscoe, *Time Bandits*

Lord, thank You for my new life, and help me to continue to grow.

WEEKEND

The Longing in Your Heart

When he was at the table with them, he took bread, gave thanks, broke it and began to give it to them. Then their eyes were opened and they recognized him, and he disappeared from their sight. They asked each other, "Were not our hearts burning within us while he talked with us on the road and opened the Scriptures to us?"

Luke 24:30–32

Everyone has a dream. It's the longing in your heart—what you would really love in life. Unless you follow your dream, you will not fulfill the destiny that God has for you.

Those who do follow their dream have to break through some areas in their life that most of us don't break through. Perhaps we don't want the dream that much; or perhaps we don't understand how a dream works.

I estimate that 85 percent of everybody I have ever met aren't following their dream. They believe they can't. And the truth of it is, every one of them can.

—Bruce Wilkinson, *The Dream Giver*

Lord, open my eyes to Your Word, and help me to break through to the vision You have for my life.

MONDAY

Good and Faithful Giving

"What good will it be for a man if he gains the whole world, yet forfeits his soul? Or what can a man give in exchange for his soul?"

Matthew 16:26

Jesus makes clear that we should do our giving to please God, not to please man. He talked about people giving so they can be seen by others. He said that if that's why you give, then that's all the reward you're going to get—the respect and appreciation and applause you get from people.

He taught a better way. *Do your giving in secret*, He said. Give to Him. Do it so that only He knows. Do it so that you're investing in His kingdom.

Are you living your life in such a way that when you stand before the Lord and He looks at your living and at your giving, He will say, *Well done, my good and faithful servant*?

—Randy Alcorn, *The Treasure Principle*

Lord, help me to hunger for Your approval, not the approval of my family, friends, workmates, and neighbors.

TUESDAY

Bitter Honey

For the lips of an adulteress drip honey, and her speech is smoother than oil;
but in the end she is bitter as gall, sharp as a double-edged sword.
Her feet go down to death; her steps lead straight to the grave.
She gives no thought to the way of life; her paths are crooked, but she knows it not.

PROVERBS 5:3–6

All of us, men and women, need affirmation. But because men actually are secretly vulnerable and may be a little insecure, it is especially important for them.

Have you ever noticed how the adulterous woman in the book of Proverbs seduces the unwitting young man? With flattery. "She took hold of him and kissed him and with a brazen face she said...'I came out to meet you; I looked for you and have found you!'" (7:13, 15) With her flattery, she enticed him and he followed her at once.

Flattery is simply a seductive counterfeit for affirmation. When a man is affirmed, he can conquer the world. But when he's not, he's sapped of his confidence. Women have an incredible opportunity to help affirm men and keep the fires burning on the home front.

—SHAUNTI FELDHAHN, *For Women Only*

Lord, help me to avoid flattery and speak truthfully
to the important people in my life.

WEDNESDAY

He Is, I Am Not

Yours, O Lord, is the greatness and the power
and the glory and the majesty and the splendor,
for everything in heaven and earth is yours.
Yours, O Lord, is the kingdom; you are exalted as head over all.

1 Chronicles 29:11

Life's moving fast today. The demands are pressing in on us from every side. We wake up. We go for it. We come to the end of the day. We always have things left on the list to do, and tomorrow we punch the button and start it all over again.

In the midst of it all, what is it all about? What does it all mean? And where do we find a sense of rest and encouragement in knowing that God is in control and in charge of everything in our lives today? I think it's in remembering that His name is *I Am that I Am*, that He is the God who is doing all things well. And remembering that our names are I Am Not. Stop for a moment today; in fact, stop for many moments today, and remember that His name is *I Am that I Am*, that He is the One who is in charge, that He can do all things and He does all things well.

—Louie Giglio, *I Am Not But I Know I Am*

Lord, thank You that You can do all things and all things well.

THURSDAY

Glow in the Dark

You, O Lord, keep my lamp burning;
my God turns my darkness into light.

Psalm 18:28

In the dark, shapes can become eerie silhouettes. True meanings are obscured. What a comfort light is. Light makes reality clear.

He who is the Light of creation says, "You are the light of the world." He's given you and me the responsibility to reveal reality in a dark, sin-blinded world. Neon toys will glow in the dark for a while if they've been exposed to enough light.

It's the same with us. The more time we spend in the presence of the Light of the world, the more we'll glow when we move into the darkness of a broken World. Take time today to step into His presence and bask in the most beautiful Light of all.

—Joni Eareckson Tada, *31 Days to Intimacy with God*

Lord, help me to remember, even if everything around me seems dark,
that You are my light and You will never go out.

FRIDAY

Honoring Our Parents

"Honor your father and your mother, so that you may live long in the land the LORD your God is giving you."

EXODUS 20:12

Sometimes the best way to honor our fathers and mothers is a simple phone call or some sort of meaningful contact. To just tell them they are special; to not ask for anything; to just say *I love you.*

But ultimately there's nothing we can do to bless them more than living a life that's righteous. If you want to bless your parents, the best thing you can do is live like a man or woman of God and live with a sense of confidence that the way you're living is putting the Lord first.

—RON MEHL, *Right with God*

Lord, help me to honor my parents,
and all my spiritual parents as well, in meaningful ways.

WEEKEND

Forgiven People

*"Why don't you judge for yourselves what is right?
As you are going with your adversary to the magistrate, try hard to be reconciled to him on the way, or he may drag you off to the judge, and the judge turn you over to the officer, and the officer throw you into prison.
I tell you, you will not get out until you have paid the last penny."*

LUKE 12:57–59

The Gospel of Matthew tells the story of the steward who owed a king a large sum he couldn't pay. Instead of sending him and his family to prison and selling them into slavery, the king decided to show mercy and forgive the steward.

Incredibly the forgiven man turned around and found a fellow servant who only owed him a small amount, a hundred *denari*. The steward refused to show compassion and had the man thrown into jail.

Christians are people who have been forgiven an incredible debt of sin against God. And unfortunately, how many of us will refuse to forgive a friend or a fellow believer or even a stranger who has committed slight offenses toward us?

—RICHARD BLACKABY, *Putting a Face on Grace*

Lord, help me to be forgiving today.

MONDAY

Uncentered on Christ

O Lord, open my lips,
and my mouth will declare your praise.
You do not delight in sacrifice, or I would bring it;
you do not take pleasure in burnt offerings.
The sacrifices of God are a broken spirit;
a broken and contrite heart,
O God, you will not despise.

Psalm 51:15–17

Here are some symptoms of not having a cross-centered life:

You are more aware of and affected by your past sin than you are the perfect and finished work of Jesus Christ. You live thinking, believing, and feeling that God is disappointed with you, rather than delighting over you. You assume that acceptance before God is dependent upon your obedience to God.

The absence of joy and the presence of condemnation is evidence that one has neglected the gospel of Jesus Christ.

—C. J. Mahaney, *Living the Cross-Centered Life*

Lord, help me to realize how much You delight in me.

TUESDAY

God Loves Nobodies

While Jesus was having dinner at Matthew's house,
many tax collectors and "sinners" came and ate with him and his disciples.
When the Pharisees saw this, they asked his disciples,
"Why does your teacher eat with tax collectors and 'sinners'?" On hearing this,
Jesus said, "It is not the healthy who need a doctor, but the sick."

Matthew 9:10–12

Do you still feel like a permanent nobody? Unremarkable and unnoticed in your life? If so, I want you to know that God especially loves nobodies.

One of my favorite nobodies was Agnes of Albania. She never went to college, never married, never owned a car. But she had a huge dream. To live out her faith to care for the dying and the poorest of poor. Most of us know her as Mother Teresa.

Whatever you feel is true or not true about you today, you were made to be someone special. Someone with a big dream beating brightly in your heart.

—Bruce Wilkinson, *The Dream Giver*

Lord, help me not to judge my value based on society,
but on Your call on my life.

WEDNESDAY

Accepting Forgiveness

This righteousness from God comes through faith in Jesus Christ to all who believe. There is no difference, for all have sinned and fall short of the glory of God, and are justified freely by his grace through the redemption that came by Christ Jesus. God presented him as a sacrifice of atonement, through faith in his blood.

Romans 3:22–25

Why is it so hard for some people to accept God's forgiveness?

One reason is because the consequences of sin may continue. The adulterer may be forgiven, but his marriage may still end in divorce. The alcoholic may be forgiven, but he has still lost his paycheck.

But perhaps the greatest reason it is difficult is because there's something within us that tells us we deserve to be punished. My friend, today I urge you quickly come to Jesus Christ. *Be forgiven.* Know that the forgiveness that He gives you is totally undeserved, but receive it with joy and gratitude. It's there for those who believe in Him.

—Erwin Lutzer, *After You've Blown It*

Lord, thank You for Your atonement.

THURSDAY

What Christ Has Planned for Us

Oh, the depth of the riches of the wisdom and knowledge of God!
How unsearchable his judgments, and his paths beyond tracing out!

Romans 11:33

A friend was selling a surfboard. I really wanted that board. So I kind of hinted around to my wife that that was what I wanted for my birthday. She said, "Oh, I've already got you something." To be honest I was kind of bummed. Then I got a card from my wife. In it were reservations for a sky-diving trip on the north shore of Hawaii. I was blown away. That board is still for sale today, but I will never again experience something like jumping out of an airplane at fifteen thousand feet in Hawaii.

It made me think. If my wife knows me that well, how much better does Christ know me? When I ask Christ for little, piddly things and say, "This is really going to make me happy, Lord," I wonder if He's thinking the same thing my wife thought. "Man, you've got no idea what I've got in store for you."

—Ryan Dobson, *2 Live 4*

Lord, thank You that You know me so well;
You know my needs better than I do.

FRIDAY

Willing to Give of Themselves

What good is it, my brothers, if a man claims to have faith but has no deeds? Can such faith save him? Suppose a brother or sister is without clothes and daily food. If one of you says to him, "Go, I wish you well; keep warm and well fed," but does nothing about his physical needs, what good is it?

JAMES 2:14–16

In 2003, college students Mike Yankoski and Sam Purvis spent more than five months living on the streets of America to learn what it means to be homeless.

On the streets of Portland we met a guy actually named Sugarman. When he found out that we were Christians, he offered everything that he owned to us, just because we believed in the Lord Jesus Christ, the same as he did. He offered his car. He offered clothes. He offered money. He said, "Whatever I can do for you, my brothers, I want to do."

Sugarman's gospel changed how he lived. That's the kind of Christianity I read of in the Gospels. That's what I see in the Bible. It's about people who love the Lord and are willing to give of themselves in order to help others. Sugarman understood that and he lived that. That was true Christianity.

—MIKE YANKOSKI, *Under the Overpass*

Lord, help me to allow the gospel to change my life.

WEEKEND

AND MARY SAID

LUKE 1:46–55

And Mary said:
"My soul glorifies the Lord and my spirit rejoices in God my Savior,
for he has been mindful of the humble state of his servant.
From now on all generations will call me blessed,
for the Mighty One has done great things for me—
holy is his name.
His mercy extends to those who fear him, from generation to generation.
He has performed mighty deeds with his arm;
he has scattered those who are proud in their inmost thoughts.
He has brought down rulers from their thrones but has lifted up the humble.
He has filled the hungry with good things but has sent the rich away empty.
He has helped his servant Israel, remembering to be merciful
to Abraham and his descendants forever, even as he said to our fathers."

Lord, thank You for Your mercy.

MONDAY

Bowing Down

Come, let us bow down in worship,
let us kneel before the LORD our Maker;
for he is our God
and we are the people of his pasture,
the flock under his care.

PSALM 95:6–7

I believe the posture of worship is important. Our physical position can affect what's going on inside us. One of the positions the Scriptures mention is bowing down. To me this is one of the most significant postures we can have.

Bowing down speaks to our heart about humbleness. It's a posture of humility, reverence, and respect, as if before a king. To bow low for someone is to me the ultimate sign of reverence and respect. And when we come before God, we should come with trembling and reverence. Bowing before our King is appropriate.

—CHRIS TOMLIN, *The Way I Was Made*

Lord, help me to bow my heart to You.

TUESDAY

SELF-PROTECTION

And God raised us up with Christ and seated us with him in the heavenly realms in Christ Jesus, in order that in the coming ages he might show the incomparable riches of his grace, expressed in his kindness to us in Christ Jesus. For it is by grace you have been saved, through faith—and this not from yourselves, it is the gift of God.

EPHESIANS 2:6–8

When I think about the term *self-protection*, I get the mental picture of somebody craving to be loved and yet wrapping their own arm around their chest to protect themselves from ever being touched or held. And in that place of self-protection there are a lot of people who are dying inside.

You see, in His grace, Jesus pursued us to the margins, to pull back the layers of self-protection. Because He knows that if we live our entire life with our hearts hidden away in the darkness, we'll simply shrivel up and die inside. And in short, He comes to us and He strips away those barriers around our hearts so that we can begin the journey out of the margins and in to reimagining our lives in His love.

—RICK MCKINLEY, *Jesus in the Margins*

Lord, thank You for Your persistent grace.

WEDNESDAY

I Know *I Am*

"O Lord, when you went out from Seir,
when you marched from the land of Edom,
the earth shook, the heavens poured,
the clouds poured down water.
The mountains quaked before the Lord, the One of Sinai,
before the Lord, the God of Israel."

Judges 5:4–5

When God told Moses on Mt. Sinai that His name was *I Am that I Am*, God was implying that He was God. *I Am the Lord. I am central. I am in control. I am everything and all that you'll ever need.* I think Moses then knew his name too. For if God's name is *I Am*, then Moses' name—and my name and yours too—must be I Am Not.

I am not God. I am not the center of the universe. I am not in control. I am a small, frail, finite man standing here having a conversation with the God of all creation. I may be I Am Not, but I know *I Am*.

—Louie Giglio, *I Am Not But I Know I Am*

Lord, thank You for being I AM.

THURSDAY

Afraid to Dream

He said, "Throw your net on the right side of the boat and you will find some." When they did, they were unable to haul the net in because of the large number of fish. Then the disciple whom Jesus loved said to Peter, "It is the Lord!"

John 21:6–7

We were talking about life dreams, and an acquaintance said, "I come from a family that doesn't seem to believe in big dreams. We were always raised to expect very little out of life. Is that why I feel so afraid to pursue my dream?"

So many people come from families and even whole cultures that don't believe in big dreams. You feel like you're walking around in a room where the ceiling is meters too low. Maybe your family made it clear without ever saying it that you're not expected to achieve much. Or maybe your family only approves of certain kinds of dreams.

What message did you receive as you were growing up? There always is a message, whether it's open or kind of beneath the surface. But God's message is this: Unless you follow your dream, you will not fulfill the destiny He has for you.

—Bruce Wilkinson, *The Dream Giver*

Lord, help me not to act in fear
and squelch Your destiny for my life.

FRIDAY

The Devil Didn't Make You Do It

For sin shall not be your master,
because you are not under law, but under grace.

Romans 6:14

Remember Flip Wilson? He was the comic whose character Geraldine was always saying, "The devil made me do it."

But it doesn't work that way. Why? Because God gave you the marvelous power of choice. The devil can entice you to do it. He can sweeten it up so you want to do it. He can make whatever it is convenient. But he cannot force your frame to do it. You must yield before you can do it.

The reason people want the devil to be at fault is so that they cannot be held responsible. No deal. If you can think and speak and function, then you're responsible. Even if your name is Geraldine.

—Tony Evans, *God Can Not Be Trusted*

Lord, thank You for grace.

WEEKEND

In Our Place

Therefore, since we are surrounded by such a great cloud of witnesses, let us throw off everything that hinders and the sin that so easily entangles, and let us run with perseverance the race marked out for us. Let us fix our eyes on Jesus, the author and perfecter of our faith, who for the joy set before him endured the cross, scorning its shame, and sat down at the right hand of the throne of God.

Hebrews 12:1–2

As a student of history, I've been astounded to read how many believers died for their faith in Jesus Christ. These martyrs seemed almost to welcome death and would often devote their dying breaths to singing.

Yet we see our Savior in Gethsemane crying out, "Oh, my Father, if it is possible, let this cup pass from me." He was not talking about physical death. He was facing something else. Something far more profound and overwhelming than anything any martyrs ever faced.

It was precisely because He faced death in these deepest dimensions that the martyrs were certain they themselves would never have to. Only by knowing this could they confront physical death with songs and shouts of victory.

—Henry Blackaby, *Experiencing the Cross*

Lord, help me to keep my eyes on You.

MONDAY

Within Relationships

Two are better than one,
because they have a good return for their work:
If one falls down,
his friend can help him up.
But pity the man who falls
and has no one to help him up!

ECCLESIASTES 4:9–10

All spiritual growth occurs within the context of relationships. We all need people close to us.

Some of our same-sex friends have become not only great friends but also crucial support for growth during difficult times. If you're going to reap the benefits of mutual accountability, then that means you and I must submit ourselves to another person who will, indeed, hold us accountable. Both a husband and a wife need at least one same-sex Christian friend if you are going to become the person God created you to be.

Don't miss the abundant life that can come when you're sharing it with a good friend.

—DENNIS AND BARBARA RAINEY, *Growing a Spiritually Strong Family*

Lord, help me to foster friendships for fun and spiritual profit.

TUESDAY

Too Wonderful for Me

Psalm 139:1–12

O Lord, you have searched me and you know me.
You know when I sit and when I rise; you perceive my thoughts from afar.
You discern my going out and my lying down; you are familiar with all my ways.
Before a word is on my tongue you know it completely, O Lord.
You hem me in—behind and before; you have laid your hand upon me.
Such knowledge is too wonderful for me, too lofty for me to attain.
Where can I go from your Spirit?
Where can I flee from your presence?
If I go up to the heavens, you are there;
if I make my bed in the depths, you are there.
If I rise on the wings of the dawn if I settle on the far side of the sea,
even there your hand will guide me, your right hand will hold me fast.
If I say, "Surely the darkness will hide me
and the light become night around me,"
even the darkness will not be dark to you;
the night will shine like the day,
for darkness is as light to you.

Lord, thank You for searching for me.

WEDNESDAY

Eternal Currency

Your wealth has rotted, and moths have eaten your clothes. Your gold and silver are corroded. Their corrosion will testify against you and eat your flesh like fire. You have hoarded wealth in the last days.

JAMES 5:2–3

Imagine that it's during the last months of the Civil War. You're a Northerner who has been living in the South and you're planning to move home. Naturally, while you've been in the South you've accumulated a fair amount of Confederate currency. But you know that the North is going to win the war, ending the Confederacy and making its money worthless.

What are you going to do with all your excess Confederate money? Well, if you're smart, there's just one answer. You keep enough to meet your short-term needs, but you think for the long term: cash it for U.S. currency, the only money that's going to have value once the war is over.

We have an opportunity when we give to the Lord's kingdom to take the stuff that's not going to last and do something with it that's going to last forever.

—RANDY ALCORN, *The Treasure Principle*

Lord, help me to be wise with what You give me and eager to serve in a way that lasts for eternity.

THURSDAY

On the Fence

Wisdom will save you from the ways of wicked men,
from men whose words are perverse,
who leave the straight paths to walk in dark ways,
who delight in doing wrong and rejoice in the perverseness of evil,
whose paths are crooked who are devious in their ways.

PROVERBS 2:12–15

You're a princess (or prince) in God's kingdom, and there are things that don't belong in a princess's life. The Bible says to guard your heart, for it affects everything that you do.

People ask me, "How did you get off drugs and make all these changes in your life?" You know what I've learned? You become what you surround yourself with. And I had to make a choice to edit the things that I read and watch and listen to. Because we cannot walk with one side in the world and one side with the Lord.

That's called riding the fence, and you get splinters in your tush.

—SHERI ROSE SHEPHERD, *My Prince Will Come*

Lord, help me to stay on the right side of the fence.

FRIDAY

The Song That Never Ends

And they cried out in a loud voice: "Salvation belongs to our God, who sits on the throne, and to the Lamb." All the angels were standing around the throne and around the elders and the four living creatures. They fell down on their faces before the throne and worshiped God, saying: "Amen! Praise and glory and wisdom and thanks and honor and power and strength be to our God for ever and ever. Amen!"

Revelation 7:10–12

When Jesus Christ hung at Calvary, He delivered us from meaningless lives into the family of God, into the love of God, into the grace of God, into the future with God. And His act was the first note in a song of praise to the God of gods. A song that's never going to end.

Now God's searching and seeking. He's looking for true worshipers. Who are they? They are the people who have moved the thing of ultimate value—which is God Himself, Creator of all things—into the center of their affections. And they have begun to live a life of worshiping Him in spirit and truth.

Are you one of them?

—Louie Giglio, *The Air I Breathe*

Lord, help me to be a true worshiper.

WEEKEND

Don't Be Afraid

They were startled and frightened, thinking they saw a ghost. [Jesus] said to them, "Why are you troubled, and why do doubts rise in your minds? Look at my hands and my feet. It is I myself! Touch me and see; a ghost does not have flesh and bones, as you see I have."

Luke 24:37–39

It's okay to be afraid when it comes to pursuing your dream. It's not okay not to do the dream.

I used to think that if God was really leading me, then I wouldn't be afraid. Then I stumbled upon the stories of Moses and Joshua. God was telling Moses to do something and Moses was scared to death, so God said, "Don't be afraid." God told Joshua very specifically what to do, and three times in two sentences He said, "Don't be afraid."

Therefore, when you hear the Word of God, you may well be afraid. But take courage! I tell myself, *I'm lifting my leg right through the wall up here, and I don't care if I am afraid, I'm going through it.* And lo and behold, before you know it, you're on the other side thinking, *What was I so afraid of*?

—Bruce Wilkinson, *The Dream Giver*

Lord, help me not to demand that You keep reassuring me, but to launch out in faith.

MONDAY

He Rules the Nations

How awesome is the Lord Most High, the great King over all the earth!
He subdued nations under us, peoples under our feet.
For God is the King of all the earth; sing to him a psalm of praise.
God reigns over the nations; God is seated on his holy throne.

Psalm 47:2–3, 7–8

Did you know that God determines every detail of every country?

He defines all boundaries. He places every milestone. While we may applaud Mayflower pilgrims and Lewis and Clark expeditions, they did nothing apart from God's power. The Bible says that He made from man every nation of mankind to live on all the face of the earth, having determined their appointed times and the boundaries of their habitation. It's God who divides His children into people groups, separates His earth into sections, and maps out the boundaries of the nations.

Every country, including ours, exists by the power of God.

—Max Lucado, *Turn*

Lord, help me to realize Your role in human history.

TUESDAY

Light of the World

He made darkness his canopy around him—
the dark rain clouds of the sky.
Out of the brightness of his presence
bolts of lightning blazed forth.
The Lord *thundered from heaven;*
the voice of the Most High resounded.

2 Samuel 22:12–14

Light is fast. If you don't believe me, just go out tonight and turn on the headlights of the car and try to race that beam of light to the driveway. Light from the sun, which is 93 million miles away, today only takes eight minutes to make that journey to reach your skin and mine. It's amazing when we think about the size of the universe. And every time we build a bigger telescope, we see something more fascinating, farther away than we've ever dreamed before.

What does it mean to us all, though, except to resize us to know that we're very small, but significant in the sense that God knows us and calls us by name. The God the Scriptures says spoke the stars into being and calls every one of them by name. And we have a place in His universe and in His story.

—Louie Giglio, *I Am Not But I Know I Am*

Lord, thank You for creating light; help me to walk in it.

WEDNESDAY

Get-Out-of-Hell-Free Card

"Now this is eternal life: that they may know you, the only true God, and Jesus Christ, whom you have sent."

John 17:3

I was at an event for broadcasters not that long ago and a friend showed me something he had developed and was really excited about. He pulled out a little yellow card that looked like the famous Get-Out-of-Jail-Free card from the Monopoly game except it said Get Out of Hell Free instead. On the back was a paragraph on how if you say certain things, you'll be a Christian.

I understood the motivation, but the idea made me a little sad. As I stared at that little yellow card, I couldn't help but think, "Is that what Christ really died for? To just die for an insurance policy?"

I think He died for something more. I think He died to give us life and life more abundant.

—Ryan Dobson, *2 Live 4*

Lord, help me to desire a relationship with You over all else.

THURSDAY

You Lifted Me Out

Psalm 40:1–3

I waited patiently for the Lord;
he turned to me and heard my cry.
He lifted me out of the slimy pit,
out of the mud and mire;
he set my feet on a rock
and gave me a firm place to stand.
He put a new song in my mouth,
a hymn of praise to our God.
Many will see and fear
and put their trust in the Lord.

Lord, I remember clearly what you brought me out of.
You are the one who set me on the rock. Now I will sing your praise!

FRIDAY

Putting Pain in Perspective

Dear friends, do not be surprised at the painful trial you are suffering, as though something strange were happening to you. But rejoice that you participate in the sufferings of Christ, so that you may be overjoyed when his glory is revealed.

1 Peter 4:12–13

"Nobody cares what I'm going through. Life will always be this hard."

When we're wounded, we need to make sure we keep pain in perspective. We want to be careful about what we say to ourselves about our wounds. Our pain, our wound, is a piece of the pie; it's not the whole pie.

We can claim a catastrophe and say things like, "This is the worst thing that could ever happen to me!" We can act like a doomsday fortune-teller: "The rest of my life is ruined and the future is hopeless."

Don't fall into this sort of attitude, It only exacerbates the problem and slows down healing.

—Dr. Steve Stephens & Pam Vredevelt, *The Wounded Woman*

Lord, help me to take the yoke You give me and learn from You.

WEEKEND

Heaven and Earth as Witnesses

Deuteronomy 30:15–20

See, I set before you today life and prosperity, death and destruction. For I command you today to love the Lord your God, to walk in his ways, and to keep his commands, decrees and laws; then you will live and increase, and the Lord your God will bless you in the land you are entering to possess. But if your heart turns away and you are not obedient, and if you are drawn away to bow down to other gods and worship them, I declare to you this day that you will certainly be destroyed. You will not live long in the land you are crossing the Jordan to enter and possess. This day I call heaven and earth as witnesses against you that I have set before you life and death, blessings and curses. Now choose life, so that you and your children may live and that you may love the Lord your God, listen to his voice, and hold fast to him. For the Lord is your life, and he will give you many years in the land he swore to give to your fathers, Abraham, Isaac and Jacob.

Lord, thank You for allowing me to choose You.

MONDAY

TARRY

I wait for the LORD, my soul waits, and in his word I put my hope.
My soul waits for the Lord more than watchmen wait for the morning,
more than watchmen wait for the morning.
O Israel, put your hope in the LORD, for with the LORD
is unfailing love and with him is full redemption.

PSALM 130:5–7

Just before Jesus Christ left the earth, He gave a command to His disciples. He said, "Go and wait—tarry—in Jerusalem until you receive the promise from on high." And then on the tenth day, a miracle began to take place.

You see, it takes perseverance if we're going to see the promises of God. Wait on the Lord, and He will give you the desire of your heart. Wait upon the Lord, and He will fulfill that which He intends for you.

—PAT ROBERTSON, *Six Steps to Spiritual Revival*

Lord, help me to wait on You for what's best for me.

TUESDAY

Dreaming Worldwide

When I was a boy in my father's house, still tender, and an only child of my mother, he taught me and said, "Lay hold of my words with all your heart; keep my commands and you will live. Get wisdom, get understanding; do not forget my words or swerve from them."

PROVERBS 4:3–5

No matter where I travel in the world, whether among Manhattan urbanites or villagers in southern Africa, I've yet to find a person who didn't have a dream. They may not be able to describe it. They may have forgotten it or no longer believe in it, but it's there.

God has put a driving passion in you to do something special. Why wouldn't He? You were created in His image. You are the only person exactly like you in the universe. And you're the only person with a dream quite like yours. You have it for a reason. To draw you toward the kind of life you were born to love.

The journey toward your big dream changes you. In fact, the journey itself is what prepares you to succeed at what you were born to do. And until you decide to pursue your dream, you're never going to love your life the way you were meant to.

—BRUCE WILKINSON, *The Dream Giver*

Lord, help me to be willing to take the next step toward Your will.

WEDNESDAY

False Promises

So I say, live by the Spirit, and you will not gratify the desires of the sinful nature. For the sinful nature desires what is contrary to the Spirit, and the Spirit what is contrary to the sinful nature. They are in conflict with each other, so that you do not do what you want.

Galatians 5:16–17

Lust uses the power of promise to deceive us. It comes to us and it says, *If you do this, you'll be happy.*

The only way we can fight those false promises of lust is to fight back with the true promises of God's Word. Think about that when lust comes to you and says something like, *Too much purity is going to keep you from seeing and enjoying beauty.*

Instead, listen to these true promises of God's Word that contradict that. Jesus said to us in Matthew 5:8, "Blessed are the pure in heart, for they will see God." In Psalm 11:7 it says, "For the Lord is righteous. He loves righteous deeds. The upright shall behold His face." These are just two examples of how Scripture gives us a better promise.

—Joshua Harris, *Sex Is Not the Problem (Lust Is)*

Lord, help me not to believe the false promises of sin; fill me with Your Spirit.

THURSDAY

Godly Desires

O God, you are my God, earnestly I seek you; my soul thirsts for you, my body longs for you, in a dry and weary land where there is no water..

Psalm 63:1

Buddhism teaches that the basic problem of life—all that happens in the cycle of karma—is that we desire things. If we did not desire things, we would not be suffering.

For instance, if you did not desire justice, you would not try to get even with someone. If you did not desire some kind of pleasure, you would not go and have that pleasure and discover that there was a cost to it and people were hurt by it. So desire is the root cause of the problem.

The truth of the matter is Jesus tells us we are to hunger for some things. For example, we are to hunger and thirst after righteousness and we shall be filled.

—Ravi Zacharias, *The Lotus and the Cross*

Lord, help me to fan the desire to seek You daily, to hunger and thirst after Your righteousness.

FRIDAY

Walking on Water

During the fourth watch of the night Jesus went out to them,
walking on the lake. When the disciples saw him walking on the lake,
they were terrified. "It's a ghost," they said, and cried out in fear.
But Jesus immediately said to them: "Take courage! It is I. Don't be afraid."
"Lord, if it's you," Peter replied, "tell me to come to you on the water."
"Come," he said.

Matthew 14:25–29

You remember the story of Peter walking on water. Peter, a human being, a fisherman, who knew the properties of water, walked on water. Surely that changed him forever. Have there been situations or events in your life in which you've walked on water? Where you knew there was no way you could do something, yet the power of Christ filled you and you did it?

Remember not the times of failure but the times you were filled with the Holy Spirit and Christ lifted you up, not on your own power, but on His.

—Ryan Dobson, *2 Live 4*

Lord, help me to walk in Your power.

WEEKEND

A Picture of God

He is the image of the invisible God, the firstborn over all creation. For by him all things were created: things in heaven and on earth, visible and invisible, whether thrones or powers or rulers or authorities; all things were created by him and for him. He is before all things, and in him all things hold together.

Colossians 1:15–17

A little boy pulled out his crayons and a sheet of paper one afternoon and began sketching. His mother asked, "What are you drawing?" And without looking up, he replied, "A picture of God." His mother smiled. "But honey, no one knows what God looks like." "Well, they will when I finish."

We smile at that story, but isn't it true that we long to see God? No one knows what He looks like. But the Nazarene, through His life and words, sketched an illustration of His Father. He drew a picture so we would know who our Father in heaven really is.

We in turn are like that little boy with his crayons. Through our words and deeds, we are sketching a picture for all to see. Our life should portray what God looks like.

—Joni Eareckson Tada, *31 Days to Intimacy with God*

Thank You, Lord Jesus, for coming to earth to be our image of God.

MONDAY

Giving and Receiving

"In everything I did, I showed you that by this kind of hard work we must help the weak, remembering the words the Lord Jesus himself said: 'It is more blessed to give than to receive.'"

Acts 20:35

Do you have all the joy and peace that you really want in your life?

Isn't that what people are looking for, joy and peace? But how do you get it?

We think it's more blessed to receive than to give. But Jesus said no, we've got it backwards. Jesus made clear how you can get joy when He said, "It is more blessed to give than to receive."

The real blessing comes when you give to someone knowing that it's going to count for eternity. And not only are you going to have the eternal benefits. Not only are you going to have joy in heaven and reward in heaven, but you can have that joy now. You can know that you're doing what you were made for. You were made to be a giver, and you know that God finds pleasure in your giving.

—Randy Alcorn, *The Treasure Principle*

Lord, help me to see opportunities to give unconditionally.

TUESDAY

God's Trustworthiness

Taste and see that the Lord is good;
blessed is the man who takes refuge in him.
Fear the Lord, you his saints,
for those who fear him lack nothing.

Psalm 34:8–9

The trustworthiness of God is all around you. Look at the consistency of creation—yes, we do have those interruptions, but look at the sun coming up and going down. Look at the changes of the leaves. Look at the consistency of how two cells come together to create a new DNA and form a new life. The Person who can do that, you can trust.

God is sovereign. That means He's in control. Even when stuff is out of control, He's in control of the out-of-controlness. Don't believe me. Put Him to the test. In fact, He says, "Try me and see whether or not I am good." Trust the Lord enough to try Him; then you'll trust Him because you'll know He is God.

—Tony Evans, *God Can Not Be Trusted*

Lord, thank You for being in control.

WEDNESDAY

Doing What It Takes

She gets up while it is still dark; she provides food for her family and portions for her servant girls.... She sets about her work vigorously; her arms are strong for her tasks. She sees that her trading is profitable, and her lamp does not go out at night.

Proverbs 31:15, 17–18

A friend once said that he always had a dream to own a business that would be successful enough to impact his hometown. "But life happened," he said. "I got a family, a job, responsibilities, all these expenses. Circumstances just didn't allow me to pursue my dream."

However, I believe that most people who truly want to pursue their dream can come up with a plan that makes a beginning possible. Of course there's a price attached. At least one sacrifice and often several. Most people who feel stuck need to rethink their priorities. Usually they have put a certain standard of living, a way of life, or some other assumption above the priority of pursuing the dream.

The minute you decide that you will do what it takes, you are already in pursuit of your dream.

—Bruce Wilkinson, *The Dream Giver*

Lord, help me to be willing to give up things if they're in the way of serving You.

THURSDAY

Forces Against the Family

Marriage should be honored by all.

Hebrews 13:4

There has never been a more difficult time to make a marriage and family work than in today's society. What are we fighting against?

First of all, there are the rotten ideas coming from the culture, like easy divorce, abortion, pervasive immorality. There's media pollution. Television shows are raunchy, and advertising is over the edge. The Internet with all of its pornographic filth is just one click away. Teenage retail stores market more than just clothing. The list goes on.

Be aware that today more than ever there are forces that want to destroy your marriage and family. Educate yourself on how to deflect them.

—Dennis and Barbara Rainey, *Growing a Spiritually Strong Family*

Lord, help me to defend marriage
as a biblical and cultural institution.

FRIDAY

Going First Class

"Which of you fathers, if your son asks for a fish, will give him a snake instead? Or if he asks for an egg, will give him a scorpion? If you then, though you are evil, know how to give good gifts to your children, how much more will your Father in heaven give the Holy Spirit to those who ask him!"

Luke 11:11–13

Have you ever gone to the airport and been told you were being upgraded to a better seat? Or have you ever checked into a hotel and been given a better room, even though you had not paid for it? You've experienced the joy of being upgraded.

As Christians we have been upgraded to a far greater degree than anyone being put into business class on an airplane. God reached down and saved us, brought us near, adopted us, gave us far more than we could have ever dreamed and certainly more than we deserve.

Anyone who truly understands what God has done for them ought to live their life in an awareness that they have been radically upgraded by God.

—Richard Blackaby, *Putting a Face on Grace*

Lord, thank You for giving me more than I could think to ask for.

WEEKEND

The Highest Value

For although they knew God, they neither glorified him as God nor gave thanks to him, but their thinking became futile and their foolish hearts were darkened.... They exchanged the truth of God for a lie, and worshiped and served created things rather than the Creator—who is forever praised.

Romans 1:21, 25

Paul says "We have traded in the Creator for the things that He has created." I see this, don't you?

Whatever we place the highest value on our lives, that's what we worship. It can be our job, or maybe a relationship. We begin to worship that. We begin to worship fame. We begin to worship popularity. We begin to worship anything that grabs our attention, instead of the One who has made all these things.

Paul says don't trade these things in. Go for the Creator, not the things He created.

—Chris Tomlin, *The Way I Was Made*

Lord, help me to focus on You, the Creator, rather than on Your created things.

MONDAY

Because We Are Loved

I pray that you, being rooted and established in love, may have power, together with all the saints, to grasp how wide and long and high and deep is the love of Christ, and to know this love that surpasses knowledge— that you may be filled to the measure of all the fullness of God.

Ephesians 3:17–19

What does God say is true about you? What does God say is true about me today?

If, in fact, God has sent His Son because He loves us, if He has pursued us through the courses of our lives because He wants to have an intimate relationship with us, then God is placing on us the highest value in the universe. He's not saying we're the most important thing in the universe, because, of course, that would be Him. But He's saying that the most important One in the universe loves us with all of His heart and has given us the greatest gift. Self-worth and God-worth merge when we see how much God loves us. Nothing on this earth that we could ever do or achieve will eclipse the value that is already ours today because we are loved and treasured by the greatest One in the whole universe.

—Louie Giglio, *I Am Not But I Know I Am*

Lord, help me to be rooted in Your love.

TUESDAY

For a Time Such as This

When Esther's words were reported to Mordecai, he sent back this answer: "Do not think that because you are in the king's house you alone of all the Jews will escape. For if you remain silent at this time, relief and deliverance for the Jews will arise from another place, but you and your father's family will perish. And who knows but that you have come to royal position for such a time as this?"

Esther 4:12–14

Because we reign as God's princesses and princes, we need to go to the Lord with our Daytimers and PDAs and calendars. We need to say, *Show me what's on here that's not of any eternal value and that You do not want me to do.*

Our time has eternal value. Think of this passage in Esther. Maybe you were appointed queen for such a time as this. We need to make sure that we don't waste the reign God has given us—that very short window to finish our faith strong.

—Sheri Rose Shepherd, *My Prince Will Come*

Lord, help me to seek Your will for my time.

WEDNESDAY

A Time for Everything

Ecclesiastes 3:1–8

There is a time for everything,
and a season for every activity under heaven:
a time to be born and a time to die,
a time to plant and a time to uproot,
a time to kill and a time to heal,
a time to tear down and a time to build,
a time to weep and a time to laugh,
a time to mourn and a time to dance,
a time to scatter stones and a time to gather them,
a time to embrace and a time to refrain,
a time to search and a time to give up,
a time to keep and a time to throw away,
a time to tear and a time to mend,
a time to be silent and a time to speak,
a time to love and a time to hate,
a time for war and a time for peace.

Lord, thank You that You have given
our existence the ebb and flow of purpose.

THURSDAY

No Fishing

He does not treat us as our sins deserve or repay us
according to our iniquities.
For as high as the heavens are above the earth,
so great is his love for those who fear him;
as far as the east is from the west,
so far has he removed our transgressions from us.

Psalm 103:10–12

One day a woman said to me, "How can I cleanse my heart?" She even added, "I cannot take steel wool to my heart and cleanse it."

The Bible says that if we confess our sins, He is faithful and just to forgive our sins. And when our sins are forgiven, they are moved as far as the east is from the west. God takes our sins. He casts them into the depths of the sea. And then He puts up a sign that says, *No fishing.*

My friend, your forgiven sin is not a problem to God. Don't let it be a problem to you.

—Erwin Lutzer, *After You've Blown It*

Lord, help me not to rehash wrongs You have forgiven me for.

FRIDAY

No Burning Bushes

I waited patiently for the Lord; he turned to me and heard my cry.
He put a new song in my mouth, a hymn of praise to our God.
Many will see and fear and put their trust in the Lord.

Psalm 40:1, 3

"Moses was lucky enough to have his dream announced to him from a burning bush," joked an acquaintance. "That hasn't happened to me. I'm in the middle of my life, and I still don't know what my big dream is supposed to be."

First, think back to what you wanted to do while you were growing up. It might have been a long list of things, including the typical firefighter or movie star or president. Think about what those roles meant to you then and what they can reveal about your real interests now. Then think about this: If someone gave you all the money you ever wanted, what would you do with it? Your answer probably reflects your dream. And lastly, ask yourself what legacy you would like to leave for your children and grandchildren. What do you want to be remembered for?

—Bruce Wilkinson, *The Dream Giver*

Lord, help me to make wise choices today.

WEEKEND

I Shall Not Want

Psalm 23

The Lord is my shepherd, I shall not be in want.
He makes me lie down in green pastures,
he leads me beside quiet waters,
he restores my soul.
He guides me in paths of righteousness for his name's sake.
Even though I walk
through the valley of the shadow of death,
I will fear no evil, for you are with me;
your rod and your staff, they comfort me.
You prepare a table before me in the presence of my enemies.
You anoint my head with oil; my cup overflows.
Surely goodness and love will follow me all the days of my life,
and I will dwell in the house of the Lord forever.

Lord, thank You for being my shepherd.

MONDAY

The Waiting Game

Therefore judge nothing before the appointed time; wait till the Lord comes.

1 Corinthians 4:5

There are days, and in fact months, when there are a million things going on. I'm on the road. I'm speaking. There are people to talk with afterwards. Then, at other times, there's nothing. It's a waiting period.

Maybe you feel that way right now. If you're out there and you've been doing all these things and then all of a sudden it's like a plateau, I want to encourage you. The waiting period is a time to rejuvenate, to refresh, to recharge your batteries. It's a time to go to a seminar, to hear a pastor, to read a book, to reread the Bible, just to sit down and pray to the Lord.

Thank Him for your period of waiting and the chance to be refreshed, and look forward to what He's got called for you in the future.

—Ryan Dobson, *2 Live 4*

Lord, help me to be patient with Your timetable.

TUESDAY

Dating the Church

But encourage one another daily, as long as it is called Today, so that none of you may be hardened by sin's deceitfulness. We have come to share in Christ if we hold firmly till the end the confidence we had at first.

Hebrews 3:13–14

I think the way a lot of people approach the local church is the way many people approach a dating relationship. I'm talking about the guy who maybe sort of likes a girl but isn't really committed. In fact, he's looking around, checking out the other alternatives.

Sadly, that's the way a lot of Christians approach involvement in the family of God. I believe that God wants for every Christian to have a passionate, committed relationship to the local church. It's in the local church that God grows us, that He uses us, that He sharpens us. That's why the local church is not something we should date. We need to settle down and get committed.

—Joshua Harris, *Stop Dating the Church*

Lord, help me to be commited to Your local body and to be an encouragement to other believers.

WEDNESDAY

Asking, Then Acting

In the same way, faith by itself, if it is not accompanied by action, is dead. But someone will say, "You have faith; I have deeds." Show me your faith without deeds, and I will show you my faith by what I do.

James 2:17–18

In 2003, college students Mike Yankoski and Sam Purvis spent more than five months living on the streets of America to learn what it means to be homeless.

We hadn't eaten in a couple of days and were growing very hungry. We started praying that God would provide something for us. These guys walked past us with a box of pizza. I asked them, "Hey, can we get the rest of that pizza? We haven't eaten today." The guy shrugged and said, "Sure. You can have it. No problem."

It's interesting that in the Old Testament, Israel asks God to provide for them. He does that through manna in the wilderness. But Israel still has to go out and pick up the manna. I think so often we pray prayers that "God, please provide for us." And yet when He does, we aren't willing to do our part.

—Mike Yankoski, *Under the Overpass*

Lord, help me to be willing to ask You for my needs and then to act.

THURSDAY

Thirsting for Meaning

Jesus answered, "Everyone who drinks this water will be thirsty again, but whoever drinks the water I give him will never thirst. Indeed, the water I give him will become in him a spring of water welling up to eternal life." The woman said to him, "Sir, give me this water so that I won't get thirsty and have to keep coming here to draw water."

John 4:13–15

I'm thirsty.

Not necessarily physically thirsty, but thirsty for meaning, meaning in my soul. When Jesus shows up in this world, He calls himself the Fountain of Living Water. He says that anyone who comes to Him and drinks will never thirst again. Can you imagine what that would be like? There are a lot of thirsty people, but it's in that place of thirst that drinking from the water of life looks most appealing. So Jesus comes to us today and invites us to come to Him and never thirst again.

—Rick McKinley, *Jesus in the Margins*

Lord, thank You for being the Living Water.

FRIDAY

Sin, Crucified

"I have been crucified with Christ and I no longer live, but Christ lives in me. The life I live in the body, I live by faith in the Son of God, who loved me and gave himself for me. I do not set aside the grace of God, for if righteousness could be gained through the law, Christ died for nothing!"

Galatians 2:20–21

Our whole identity in Christ is found in the cross. It was there that God dealt totally and radically with sin.

In our intimate relationship with Christ and His crucifixion, God intends for us to see sin as He does and to feel the horrors of sin as Christ did. He wants us to therefore let the Father crucify sin in our lives, just as He crucified His own Son. He wants us to literally die to sin and never again know it as a way of life.

Knowing this—that our old man was crucified with Him, that the body of sin might be done away with—we should no longer be slaves of sin.

—Henry Blackaby, *Experiencing the Cross*

Lord, help me to comprehend how sin hurts You and how I am no longer a slave to it.

WEEKEND

All We Like Sheep

"What do you think? If a man owns a hundred sheep, and one of them wanders away, will he not leave the ninety-nine on the hills and go to look for the one that wandered off?"

Matthew 18:12

When we think of a shepherd, we may picture somebody just standing on a hill, watching his sheep lying around him. What we don't see is the close connection between the two. You see, a sheep is totally dependent on a good shepherd because sheep are dumb by nature.

Well, we are spiritually dumb, so we need an intelligent shepherd too. Doesn't the Bible say, "All we like sheep have gone astray"? You don't get a better shepherd than God Almighty. So when we humble ourselves, acknowledge ourselves to be like sheep, and give Him the right to be Shepherd, well, now we're on our way to getting to our destination.

—Tony Evans, *God Is More than Enough*

Lord, help me to humble myself daily and remember that I am dependent upon the Shepherd.

MONDAY

Never Too Late

Sing to the Lord a new song; sing to the Lord, all the earth.
Sing to the Lord, praise his name; proclaim his salvation day after day.
Declare his glory among the nations, his marvelous deeds among all peoples.
For great is the Lord and most worthy of praise; he is to be feared above all gods.

Psalm 96:1–4

A man I know realizes now that he went into business because it seemed logical at the time. "Perhaps if I had had the time to learn how to dream earlier, I would have seen that something like engineering would be the path to go."

However, I told him that while you have breath, it's never too late to act on your dream. Your dream may not look quite the same as it did years ago, but the essence of the dream, the tug of longing you feel to do what God made you to do is still there. No matter what's happened in your past or what circumstance you're in, you can turn your heart toward your dream starting now.

—Bruce Wilkinson, *The Dream Giver*

Lord, help me to seek Your perfect plan for my life today.

TUESDAY

MARK OF A CHRISTIAN

And we, who with unveiled faces all reflect the Lord's glory,
are being transformed into his likeness with ever-increasing glory,
which comes from the Lord, who is the Spirit.

2 CORINTHIANS 3:18–19

Uniforms can give otherwise average-looking people a look of dignity. However, it doesn't come without a cost, does it?

People in the military go through intense training. They earn the right to put on the clothing they wear. *Awright, Briscoe. That's it. Give me twenty.*

Maybe you're not in the military, but if you call yourself a Christian, there's a lot attached to that. Unfortunately, there's no shortage of folks in the church who don't take their calling seriously. As a result, they make bad choices—they tarnish the uniform.

The Christian life isn't just about looking. But if we've been transformed by God's kindness, our attitudes and priorities should be ones of obedience, not rebellion. If we profess, we need to practice. It's a priority for a person who wears the uniform of the kingdom.

—STUART BRISCOE, *Time Bandits*

Lord, help me to "put on" Your uniform of love.

WEDNESDAY

He Will Bind Up Our Wounds

Hosea 6:1–3

"Come, let us return to the Lord.
He has torn us to pieces
but he will heal us;
he has injured us
but he will bind up our wounds.
After two days he will revive us;
on the third day he will restore us,
that we may live in his presence.
Let us acknowledge the Lord;
let us press on to acknowledge him.
As surely as the sun rises,
he will appear;
he will come to us like the winter rains,
Like the spring rains that water the earth."

Lord, thank You for reviving us.

THURSDAY

The Payoff That Counts

The sluggard's craving will be the death of him, because his hands refuse to work. All day long he craves for more, but the righteous give without sparing.

Proverbs 21:25–26

Years ago I traveled to the ancient country of Egypt. While there I visited two graves.

One was that of William Borden, an American missionary who gave up everything—his was from a very wealthy family—and ended up serving only briefly as a missionary before dying of spinal meningitis at twenty-five.

The other grave belonged to someone who also died young: King Tutankhamen. King Tut tried to take all those tons of gold treasures with him. But, of course, he had to leave them behind.

William Borden, on the other hand, got it right. The gravestone at his grave site says, *Apart from faith in Christ, there is no explanation for such a life*. Borden is now experiencing in eternity the payoff for the giving he did while on earth.

—Randy Alcorn, *The Treasure Principle*

Lord, help me to give without sparing, even my own life.

FRIDAY

Real Intimacy

Therefore, my brothers, be all the more eager to make your calling and election sure. For if you do these things, you will never fall, and you will receive a rich welcome into the eternal kingdom of our Lord and Savior Jesus Christ.

2 Peter 1:10–11

Imagine you're slumped on the couch watching a mindless sitcom, and during the commercial the Spirit whispers, "Turn it off and spend a few moments with Me." How do you respond? Or say you're tossing and turning in bed, fretful, and you can't get to sleep. And out of nowhere, the Spirit says, "Why don't you use this time to pray?" Will you do it?

God loves to break in beyond the structured minutes you have scheduled for Him. To be honest, those are often the times when real intimacy with God begins. Trust can only increase when we redeem inopportune moments as ways to know Him better. In the midst of an anxious day or worry-torn night, the Holy Spirit wants to flood your soul with His hope and joy. Ask Him to do that today.

—Joni Eareckson Tada, *31 Days to Intimacy with God*

Lord, help me respond to Your invitations.

WEEKEND

Never Thirsty Again

John 4:7–14

When a Samaritan woman came to draw water, Jesus said to her,
"Will you give me a drink?" (His disciples had gone into the town to buy food.)
The Samaritan woman said to him, "You are a Jew
and I am a Samaritan woman. How can you ask me for a drink?"
(For Jews do not associate with Samaritans.)
Jesus answered her, "If you knew the gift of God and who it is that asks you
for a drink, you would have asked him and he would have given you living water."
"Sir," the woman said, "you have nothing to draw with and the well is deep.
Where can you get this living water?
Are you greater than our father Jacob, who gave us the well and drank
from it himself, as did also his sons and his flocks and herds?"
Jesus answered, "Everyone who drinks this water will be thirsty again,
but whoever drinks the water I give him will never thirst. Indeed, the water I
give him will become in him a spring of water welling up to eternal life."

Heavenly Father, may I continually overflow with Your abundant life.

MONDAY

What Controls You?

This righteousness from God comes through faith in Jesus Christ to all who believe. There is no difference, for all have sinned and fall short of the glory of God, and are justified freely by his grace through the redemption that came by Christ Jesus.

Romans 3:22–24

We all have pain and problems. We all have weaknesses. We all fall short of God's glory. And you know what? We don't need to hide it, we need to heal it. I have found that if we do not find the root of what's causing us to react or act a certain way, it finds us.

You know how it finds us? It finds us in exhaustion, eating addiction, fear, depression, illness. Remember what Peter said? "A man is a slave to whatever has mastered him" (2 Peter 2:19).

So get with the Lord with a blank piece of paper, and write down your issues. When you write something down, it becomes real. Then go to the Word.

—Sheri Rose Shepherd, *My Prince Will Come*

Lord, help me to see Your grace in the areas of my life where I fall short of Your glory.

TUESDAY

How God Meets Our Needs

The body is a unit, though it is made up of many parts; and though all its parts are many, they form one body. So it is with Christ. For we were all baptized by one Spirit into one body—whether Jews or Greeks, slave or free—and we were all given the one Spirit to drink.

1 Corinthians 12:12–13

Maybe friends keep telling you to go to church but you wonder, *Isn't knowing God enough?*

True, God is "enough." He's given us His Holy Spirit and His Word. And yet what is also true is that God has chosen to use other people to be a means of His transformation in our life.

He's chosen to use people that sometimes rub us the wrong way to help us see our hearts. When we need a helping hand, God extends His love to us through fellow brothers and sisters in Christ who demonstrate God's love. This way not only are our needs met, but God's goodness and provision is demonstrated, bringing Him glory.

—Joshua Harris, *Stop Dating the Church*

Lord, thank You for the others in my life
You've chosen to help me grow.

WEDNESDAY

God-Given Dreams

Strengthen the feeble hands, steady the knees that give way; say to those with fearful hearts, "Be strong, do not fear; your God will come."

Isaiah 35:3–4

What keeps people from embracing and pursuing their God-given dreams? I've noticed five common, but critical, misconceptions.

Number one, thinking I don't have a dream. Two, thinking I have to invent my dream. Three, thinking I have a dream but it's not that important. Four, thinking I have a dream but it's up to God to make it happen. And five, thinking I had a dream but it's too late.

Take a minute to check out your own beliefs. Think about those statements carefully. Do any of them describe your beliefs about a big dream for your life? If you're not sure, at least take a moment and look at your actions. What you do is usually a result of what you actually believe.

—Bruce Wilkinson, *The Dream Giver*

Lord, help me to replace any wrong beliefs that stop me from serving You.

THURSDAY

No Time, No Time

Do not be in a hurry to leave the king's presence.

Ecclesiastes 8:3

Let me ask you a question. Are you in a hurry right now? Perhaps a better question would be, do you live a hurried lifestyle? A good friend of mine once said to me, "To say that you don't have time is not a statement of fact, but a statement of value."

When we live a hurried lifestyle, we have little time for serious spiritual reflection. There's little time to share dreams and needs with other members of the body of Christ. And if you're part of a couple, there's little time to share lives with one another.

Take time today to carve out time for what's important.

—Dennis and Barbara Rainey, *Pressure Proof Your Marriage*

Lord, help me to slow down my life.

FRIDAY

Innocent Before God

Meanwhile Jesus stood before the governor, and the governor asked him, "Are you the king of the Jews?"

"Yes, it is as you say," Jesus replied.

When he was accused by the chief priests and the elders, he gave no answer. Then Pilate asked him, "Don't you hear the testimony they are bringing against you?" But Jesus made no reply, not even to a single charge—to the great amazement of the governor.

MATTHEW 27:11–14

Most of us, when falsely accused, will try to vindicate our innocence. But Jesus did not. Why do you think He responded this way? Why would He keep quiet?

We find the answer when we see this moment from God's perspective. Jesus sought approval from One and One only—His Father in heaven. And He knew that before God He was absolutely innocent. So why bother discussing it or defending it with people? Why waste words? Why play their game?

As long as God knows, that is enough.

—HENRY BLACKABY, *Experiencing the Cross*

Lord, help me to rest in Your omniscient knowledge.

WEEKEND

Free from Nagging Guilt

The Spirit and the bride say, "Come!" And let him who hears say, "Come!" Whoever is thirsty, let him come; and whoever wishes, let him take the free gift of the water of life.

Revelation 22:17

Counseling people has made me realize that people try to deal with their guilt in so many different ways, such as alcohol and drugs. We will do anything to try to overcome guilt. I want you to know today that God is the only One who has a detergent that can scrub our consciences clean.

I encourage you to come to Jesus Christ today no matter how badly you've blown it. Rush to Him. Confess your sin. Acknowledge Him as your Savior, and be free from the nagging guilt that leads you to despair.

—Erwin Lutzer, *After You've Blown It*

Lord, thank You for your invitation to the free gift of the water of life.

MONDAY

TRULY BLESSED

MATTHEW 5:3–10

"Blessed are the poor in spirit,
for theirs is the kingdom of heaven.
Blessed are those who mourn,
for they will be comforted.
Blessed are the meek,
for they will inherit the earth.
Blessed are those who hunger and thirst for righteousness,
for they will be filled.
Blessed are the merciful,
for they will be shown mercy.
Blessed are the pure in heart,
for they will see God.
Blessed are the peacemakers,
for they will be called sons of God.
Blessed are those who are persecuted because of righteousness,
for theirs is the kingdom of heaven."

Lord Jesus, help me to walk the path of true happiness,
not in the ways of this world.

TUESDAY

THE ETERNITY PRIZE

Everyone who competes in the games goes into strict training. They do it to get a crown that will not last; but we do it to get a crown that will last forever. Therefore I do not run like a man running aimlessly; I do not fight like a man beating the air. No, I beat my body and make it my slave so that after I have preached to others, I myself will not be disqualified for the prize.

1 CORINTHIANS 9:25–27

All athletes practice strict self-control. But they do it to win a prize that will fade away. You, however, do it for an eternal prize. You see the difference?

Nevertheless, life is hard, isn't it? The devil loves nothing more than when Christians are too tired to pray, too tired to work on their marriages, too tired to deal with their children. His greatest victory is when we're in a coma, when our brain is not on and alert and self-controlled.

We need to ask God to help us with energy and self-control.

—SHERI ROSE SHEPHERD, *My Prince Will Come*

Lord, help me to make my body my slave.

WEDNESDAY

True Fellowship

God has combined the members of the body and has given greater honor to the parts that lacked it, so that there should be no division in the body, but that its parts should have equal concern for each other. If one part suffers, every part suffers with it; if one part is honored, every part rejoices with it.

1 Corinthians 12:24–26

Okay, you ready for a great Christian cliché? Fellowship. We are so used to this word, aren't we? *Fellowship halls.* "Let's have a little fellowship time." Two Christians eating donuts, *fellowshipping.*

Yet what does fellowship really mean? Well, fellowship is sharing together the life made possible by the Holy Spirit living within us. The Christian life is a life that's meant to be shared. We are to walk out the Christian life, side by side, arms locked together, where we're talking about what God is doing in us and through us. It's where real growth takes place, where real transformation takes place.

That's why the local church is so important. We need fellowship. Not just a cliché. The real deal.

—Joshua Harris, *Stop Dating the Church*

Lord, help me to make fellowship a priority.

THURSDAY

From Grief to Glory

Why are you downcast, O my soul?
Why so disturbed within me?
Put your hope in God,
for I will yet praise him,
my Savior and my God.

Psalm 42:11

There are times for all of us when we wonder, *Will this pain ever end*?

After our (Pam) first baby died and after our third child was born with severe handicaps and Down Syndrome, I suffered such tremendous turmoil and grief. I wondered if this pain, the ache I physically felt in my heart, would ever go away.

But God is faithful. God will get you through those times. He will take those difficulties and use them as opportunities to move you forward in His plans and purposes. He will take those difficult traumas, whatever this world delivers, and work them for your highest good and His greatest glory.

—Dr. Steve Stephens & Pam Vredevelt, *The Wounded Woman*

Lord, thank You for the promise of hope during difficult times.

FRIDAY

Obstacles Are Opportunities

We also rejoice in our sufferings, because we know that suffering produces perseverance; perseverance, character; and character, hope. And hope does not disappoint us, because God has poured out his love into our hearts by the Holy Spirit, whom he has given us.

ROMANS 5:3–5

Perhaps you have a dream right now, but it seems impossible to pursue. Or, are you pursuing your dream, but experiencing setback after setback?

All dreamers soon learn that the road to the future they really want is clogged with dream-threatening obstacles. That's why so many turn back. But what many don't realize—and what I missed for many years—is that each obstacle is also an important opportunity. The better you understand the journey to your dream and what God is doing in your life, the less likely you are to abandon your dream.

Your dream is yours to act on. God is waiting for you to value His gift of your dream enough to live it. He will not force you to choose. Nor will He make it happen for you. You must choose. You must act.

—BRUCE WILKINSON, *The Dream Giver*

Lord, help me to view obstacles as opportunities for faith growth.

WEEKEND

Delight in the Lord

Trust in the Lord and do good; dwell in the land and enjoy safe pasture.
Delight yourself in the Lord and he will give you the desires of your heart.
Commit your way to the Lord; trust in him and he will do this.

Psalm 37:3–5

For years Psalm 37:4 was like my life verse. I had intense desires. I loved music and I wanted to play, so I thought, *God, Your promise is to give me the desires of my heart....* But I would always skip over the first part! "Delight yourself in the Lord...."

What does it mean to delight yourself in the Lord? It simply means to treasure what God treasures. And to walk with Him and to know Him. To commune with Him. To have a relationship with Him. To delight yourself in Him, just like you would delight yourself in the love of your life.

Then when you begin to delight yourself in Him, His desires become your desires.

—Chris Tomlin, *The Way I Was Made*

Lord, help me to delight in You.

MONDAY

Majestic

Psalm 8

O Lord, our Lord, how majestic is your name in all the earth!
You have set your glory above the heavens.
From the lips of children and infants you have ordained praise
because of your enemies, to silence the foe and the avenger.
When I consider your heavens, the work of your fingers,
the moon and the stars, which you have set in place,
what is man that you are mindful of him,
the son of man that you care for him?
You made him a little lower than the heavenly beings
and crowned him with glory and honor.
You made him ruler over the works of your hands;
you put everything under his feet:
all flocks and herds, and the beasts of the field,
the birds of the air,
and the fish of the sea, all that swim the paths of the seas.
O Lord, our Lord,
how majestic is your name in all the earth!

Lord, thank You for being mindful of me.

TUESDAY

Turning to God

If my people, who are called by my name, will humble themselves and pray
and seek my face and turn from their wicked ways,
then will I hear from heaven and will forgive their sin and will heal their land.

2 Chronicles 7:14

God's definition of the family has come under question, even ridicule. Freedom of speech is guaranteed to students, unless the topic is religious. A movement to remove the phrase *Under God* from the Pledge of Allegiance gained momentum before being dismissed on a technicality. A vocal portion of the American populace stares at the strand of faith upon which this country hangs and asks, "Why is that there?"

What stirs God to heal a land? What conditions trigger refreshing rains? What prompts the Almighty to cure a country? The answer lies in the word *turn.*

God asks us to turn—to turn from self-promotion to God-promotion, from self-reliance to God-dependence, from self-direction to God-direction, to turn from self-service to repentance. When will God heal the land? When the people turn back to Him.

—Max Lucado, *Turn*

Lord, help me to turn to You and to pray
for my neighbors, community, and country to do the same.

WEDNESDAY

THE HINDRANCE OF LEGALISM

Again, the gift of God is not like the result of the one man's sin: The judgment followed one sin and brought condemnation, but the gift followed many trespasses and brought justification. For if, by the trespass of the one man, death reigned through that one man, how much more will those who receive God's abundant provision of grace and of the gift of righteousness reign in life through the one man, Jesus Christ.

ROMANS 5:16–17

Legalism is a primary hindrance to a cross-centered life. I define legalism as seeking to achieve forgiveness from God, justification before God, and acceptance by God through our obedience to God. Legalism means that we consider the cross of Christ insufficient. Legalism is substituting our works for His finished work. Legalism is self-atonement for the purpose of self-glorification and ultimately self-worship.

A cross-centered life has nothing to do with legalism.

—C. J. MAHANEY, *Living the Cross-Centered Life*

Lord, help me to realize that I am free in You.

THURSDAY

The Mind of a Sheep

Jesus went through all the towns and villages, teaching in their synagogues, preaching the good news of the kingdom and healing every disease and sickness. When he saw the crowds, he had compassion on them, because they were harassed and helpless, like sheep without a shepherd.

Matthew 9:35–36

Sheep are not independent animals. They are totally dependent on their shepherd. A sheep who misunderstands its "sheepness" and wanders away from the shepherd is lost.

You and I are sheep. We need to look to our Shepherd for everything. Yet many Christians have lost their "sheepness," their sense of who they are. They view themselves as independent and self-sufficient. *God is only good for emergencies. Up until then, I can handle things myself.*

That is idolatry and why we don't experience more of the divine. You must take the mindset of a sheep to get the benefits of the Shepherd.

—Tony Evans, *God Is More than Enough*

Lord, help me not to forget that You are the Shepherd and I am the sheep.

FRIDAY

The Words of My Mouth

May the words of my mouth and the meditation of my heart be pleasing in your sight, O Lord, my Rock and my Redeemer.

Psalm 19:14

Have you ever heard a comment like this?

"Hey, do you really want to go to that church fellowship thing? It puts me to sleep. I hate missing half of my favorite Wednesday night show. I mean, can we get Tivo or something?"

I've known people who were appalled at learning just how many negative words they were saying. I go as far as calling them words of death.

The opposite are grace words. There are a lot of ways that you can cultivate grace words in your own vocabulary. Start by auditing what is coming out of your mouth.

—Richard Blackaby, *Putting a Face on Grace*

Lord, help me to guard my mouth and fill my conversation with words of grace.

WEEKEND

A Father's Provision

And my God will meet all your needs
according to his glorious riches in Christ Jesus..

Philippians 4:19

I love the commandment *Thou shall not steal* because it's a constant reminder of God's great love for us.

How would I feel if my two young sons felt they had to provide their own clothes and food and shelter? I would really be embarrassed as a father. That's my job, taking care of my children.

Well, one reason God says don't steal is because it's His "job" to take care of us. "Why would you want to steal anything," He asks, "when I've already promised you that I'm going to provide for you everything you're ever going to need?" If we don't believe it, then we don't trust Him.

—Ron Mehl, *Right with God*

Lord, thank You that as my heavenly Father
You will never neglect me; I will never have an excuse to steal.

MONDAY

Because He Knew Us

My frame was not hidden from you when I was made in the secret place. When I was woven together in the depths of the earth, your eyes saw my unformed body. All the days ordained for me were written in your book before one of them came to be.

Psalm 139:15–16

In the book of Jeremiah, chapter 1, verses 4–5, it says this: "Then the Word of the Lord came to me saying, 'Before I formed you in the womb, I knew you.'"

Wait a minute. Before God formed you and me in the womb, He knew us? How could He know us before we existed? *Because* He knew us—*that's why He formed us the way He did!*

Wait a minute. How could He know us before we were? Because He's God. Remember, He's not bound by time. We're caught in time—and not much time at that—but there is no time in heaven.

But back to the point: He formed us the way He did because he knew what He planned for us. Isn't that amazing?

—Bruce Wilkinson, *The Dream Giver*

Lord, thank You for loving me even before I was born.

TUESDAY

Reason to Rejoice

"[The rich man] said, 'This is what I'll do. I will tear down my barns and build bigger ones, and there I will store all my grain and my goods. And I'll say to myself, "You have plenty of good things laid up for many years. Take life easy; eat, drink and be merry."' But God said to him, 'You fool! This very night your life will be demanded from you. Then who will get what you have prepared for yourself?' This is how it will be with anyone who stores up things for himself but is not rich toward God."

LUKE 12:18–21

Our tendency is to accumulate earthly things. They become our center of gravity. Jesus says switch your center of gravity—from earth to heaven.

If your treasures are on earth, every day of your life you're walking away from them. But if your treasures are in heaven, every day you're walking toward them.

The person who spends his life headed away from his treasures has reason to despair. The person who spends his life heading toward his treasures has reason to rejoice.

—RANDY ALCORN, *The Treasure Principle*

Lord, help me not to accumulate things and think myself rich.

WEDNESDAY

The Good Life

"The thief comes only to steal and kill and destroy; I have come that they may have life, and have it to the full."

John 10:10

One of the ways in which we look at life and determine whether our lives are good or bad is often through economic things, material things, and relational things.

We look on the TV and see people in mansions and people in new cars, and we think to ourselves, *They're living the good life.* Christ came into the world to redefine what the good life really is. The good life not being about toys and accumulation of things, but the good life being one in which you are loved by the Father, forgiven by the Son, and sealed with the Holy Spirit. As Jesus comes to us in the margins, He comes to us ready to redefine where the good life is and invite us to take the next step with Him in that place.

—Rick McKinley, *Jesus in the Margins*

Lord, help me to realize what a "good life" really is.

THURSDAY

Needing and Wanting

I know what it is to be in need, and I know what it is to have plenty. I have learned the secret of being content in any and every situation, whether well fed or hungry, whether living in plenty or in want.

PHILIPPIANS 4:12

In *2003, college students Mike Yankoski and Sam Purvis spent more than five months living on the streets of America to learn what it means to be homeless.*

About two days after we got off the streets in November, we stopped at a bookstore. Now I had a wallet in my pocket with a little piece of plastic. I suddenly wanted to own everything in the store.

Understanding the difference between needing and wanting is critical in our lives if we are to be good stewards of the things that we have.

The best meal I've ever eaten was when I was very hungry. The best rest I've ever had was when I was exhausted. And yet I run around trying to fill those needs—trying to never be hungry and never be tired—even though we appreciate things more when we don't instantly gratify those desires.

—MIKE YANKOSKI, *Under the Overpass*

Lord, help me to remember the difference between needs and wants.

FRIDAY

The Most Important

The one who calls you is faithful and he will do it.

1 Thessalonians 5:24

You've probably had a similar exchange:

"What are you doing today?"

"Well, I have to volunteer in the church office, stop by the post office, go to the library, do some laundry, walk the dogs, pay some bills, and then get to school by three-thirty."

"So, the usual."

"Yeah."

When Jesus said seek first the kingdom and all these things shall be added to you, He wasn't saying that everything besides the kingdom was unimportant, only less important. Sometimes, though, at the end of the day, what we say is important and what we've actually spent all our time on are two different things.

God is aware of everything you've got going on. It's time to trust Him with all of it.

—Stuart Briscoe, *Time Bandits*

Lord, help me to trust You for all the daily details.

WEEKEND

Where the Wind Blows

"You should not be surprised at my saying, 'You must be born again.' The wind blows wherever it pleases. You hear its sound, but you cannot tell where it comes from or where it is going. So it is with everyone born of the Spirit."

John 3:7–8

The Carpenter must have paused in the conversation, feeling a cool evening breeze on His face. "The wind," He told the Pharisee, "blows wherever it pleases. You hear its sound, but you cannot tell where it comes from or where it is going. So it is with everyone born of the Spirit."

Wind. By its very nature, it moves. And just so, the Spirit never lies dormant. He's always making His presence known, where He wills. Although we cannot see the wind, we know it moves by its effect. Think of waving trees and flowers or smoke from a fire. In its wake, the wind leaves freshness and cleansing.

As you allow the Spirit to fill and empower your life, others will mark His presence. Breath deeply of His fragrance and give thanks.

—Joni Eareckson Tada, *31 Days to Intimacy with God*

Lord, help me to listen for Your movement and respond to Your nudges.

MONDAY

The Perfect Law

Psalm 19:7–14

The law of the Lord is perfect, reviving the soul.
The statutes of the Lord are trustworthy, making wise the simple.
The precepts of the Lord are right, giving joy to the heart.
The commands of the Lord are radiant, giving light to the eyes.
The fear of the Lord is pure, enduring forever.
The ordinances of the Lord are sure and altogether righteous.
They are more precious than gold, than much pure gold;
they are sweeter than honey, than honey from the comb.
By them is your servant warned; in keeping them there is great reward.
Who can discern his errors? Forgive my hidden faults.
Keep your servant also from willful sins; may they not rule over me.
Then will I be blameless, innocent of great transgression.
May the words of my mouth and
the meditation of my heart be pleasing in your sight,
O LORD, *my Rock and my Redeemer.*

Lord, thank You for Your perfect law.

TUESDAY

Time for Courage

Better a dry crust with peace and quiet than
a house full of feasting, with strife.

Proverbs 17:1

If you're like most Americans, you're overcommitted, sleep-deprived, frazzled, running on empty—and longing for just five minutes alone with no one bugging you.

Pressure is the number one silent killer in most relationships in this country. People do not carve out the time to rest and reflect, let alone communicate with one another. It's especially hard for couples.

What's needed today as we face the relentless pace of life is heroic, hill-charging courage—courage to make some choices that demand personal self-sacrifice. Are you willing to be courageous today and face down the pressures of your life?

—Dennis and Barbara Rainey, *Pressure Proof Your Marriage*

Lord, help me decide to stop letting
pressure and busyness ruin my relationships.

WEDNESDAY

What You Do Best

Do not tremble, do not be afraid. Did I not proclaim this and foretell it long ago? You are my witnesses. Is there any God besides me? No, there is no other Rock; I know not one.

Isaiah 44:8

An allegorical tale of a character named Ordinary from the town of Familiar:

The night before he left Familiar, Ordinary decided to use the long, white feather to help him remember the truth. He pulled out a notebook and wrote *My Dream Journal* on the cover. Then he dipped the quill in permanent ink and wrote on the first page.

"The Dream Giver gave me a big dream before I was even born. I just finally woke up to it. My dream is what I do best. And what I most love to do. How could I have missed it for so long? I have to sacrifice and make big changes to pursue my dream, but it will be worth it. It makes me sad to think that so many Nobodies are missing something so big."

—Bruce Wilkinson, *The Dream Giver*

Lord, thank You that You created me able to dream.

THURSDAY

Passion for the Church

Now the Bereans were of more noble character than the Thessalonians, for they received the message with great eagerness and examined the Scriptures every day to see if what Paul said was true.

Acts 17:11

We all are passionate about something. What about you? What is it that you love to talk about, that you love to think about, that you love to give your free time to? Put your finger on that thing, and that's an example of passion.

The question that I want to ask each one of us as Christians is, are we passionate about the family of God? Are we willing to give it our time? Are we willing to invest our gifts in it? Are we willing to dream about it and think about it and ask how can I make this more successful for God's glory?

All these are ways in which we can make the church our passion.

—Joshua Harris, *Stop Dating the Church*

Lord, help me to be passionate about Your church and to search the Scriptures for ways to help Your family grow.

FRIDAY

The Perspective of Scripture

Those who live according to the sinful nature have their minds set on what that nature desires; but those who live in accordance with the Spirit have their minds set on what the Spirit desires.

Romans 8:5

As long as we know the Scripture, we don't have to be slaves to our emotional reactions when we confront difficult situations or difficult people. We can respond, instead, as God's Word tells us to.

Jesus grasped fully the message and promise of Scripture. And because He trusted His Father and remained yielded and obedient to His will, He knew that death, even deepest death, would not be the end of the story. The horror and anguish would be followed by the glory of His promised resurrection and the final accomplishment of God's plan and purpose for redemption.

If you don't know the Scripture, however, you'll simply act as the world acts. You'll do what you're used to always doing in the flesh.

—Henry Blackaby, *Experiencing the Cross*

Lord, help me to bring my feelings captive to Your Word.

WEEKEND

Wise, Not Rich

Proverbs 8:1, 4–10

Does not wisdom call out?
Does not understanding raise her voice?...
"To you, O men, I call out;
I raise my voice to all mankind.
You who are simple, gain prudence;
you who are foolish, gain understanding.
Listen, for I have worthy things to say;
I open my lips to speak what is right.
My mouth speaks what is true,
for my lips detest wickedness.
All the words of my mouth are just;
none of them is crooked or perverse.
To the discerning all of them are right;
they are faultless to those who have knowledge.
Choose my instruction instead of silver,
knowledge rather than choice gold.

Oh, Lord, teach me to listen intently to You and Your Word.
Help me to desire and seek Your wisdom more than wealth.

MONDAY

The Fame of God

Lord, I have heard of your fame;
I stand in awe of your deeds, O Lord.
Renew them in our day,
in our time make them known;
in wrath remember mercy.

Habakkuk 3:2

This verse in the book of Habakkuk has always stood out to me. We have heard of Your fame. We stand in awe of Your deeds. Renew them in our day.

I think that's what we're here for. We are here for one thing, and that is to feel the fame of God. Not to make ourselves famous, but to make God famous in every way, in everything we do in all of our lives to bring Him the glory. And I believe when we do that, we're fulfilling why we were created—to be His people who proclaim His name in our day.

May that be our prayer, that we would renew the fame of God in our day.

—Chris Tomlin, *The Way I Was Made*

Lord, help me to spread Your fame.

TUESDAY

Listen to Grandma

When I said, "My foot is slipping," your love, O Lord, supported me.
When anxiety was great within me, your consolation brought joy to my soul.

Psalm 94:18–19

When I'm fearful or anxious, I just don't think very well. I think some of the goofiest things, and I get into negative thinking.

When the anxiety comes, I need to say, "Okay, what is reality, and why am I assuming the worst?" A lot of times the stuff I worry about never happens.

Besides, as my grandma told me years ago, we need to ask ourselves, "What difference will this make in ten years?"

God can make something wonderful out of our biggest mess-ups anyway.

—Dr. Steve Stephens & Pam Vredevelt, *The Wounded Woman*

Lord, help me not to assume the worst but
to move ahead, trusting in You.

WEDNESDAY

Justification and Sanctification

For it is by grace you have been saved, through faith—and this not from yourselves, it is the gift of God—not by works, so that no one can boast. For we are God's workmanship, created in Christ Jesus to do good works, which God prepared in advance for us to do..

Ephesians 2:8–10

For every Christian, legalism is a daily temptation and tendency.

We are particularly vulnerable to legalism if we do not distinguish between justification and sanctification. Justification is our position before God. Sanctification is our practice before God. Justification is a pronouncement. Sanctification is a process.

Actually, you will never be more justified before God than you are the first moment you trust in the person and finished word of Jesus Christ. Nothing we ever do contributes to the basis of our justification.

—C. J. Mahaney, *Living the Cross-Centered Life*

Lord, help me to realize how I stand before Your throne.

THURSDAY

Lift My Eyes

Psalm 121

I lift up my eyes to the hills—
where does my help come from?
My help comes from the Lord,
the Maker of heaven and earth.
He will not let your foot slip—
he who watches over you will not slumber;
indeed, he who watches over Israel
will neither slumber nor sleep.
The Lord watches over you—
the Lord is your shade at your right hand;
the sun will not harm you by day,
nor the moon by night.
The Lord will keep you from all harm—
he will watch over your life;
the Lord will watch over your coming and going
both now and forevermore.

Lord, thank You for watching over me!

FRIDAY

Out of the Comfort Zone

But the LORD said to me, "Do not say, 'I am only a child.' You must go to everyone I send you to and say whatever I command you. Do not be afraid of them, for I am with you and will rescue you," declares the LORD. Then the LORD reached out his hand and touched my mouth and said to me, "Now, I have put my words in your mouth."

JEREMIAH 1:7–9

The trouble with our life dreams is that they're *over there.* They're in a place we have never been. It's unknown. And most of us, if not all of us, think that the territory between the dream and its fulfillment is a vague, murky, uncertain, uncharted, illogical, haphazard journey. We don't realize that there are stages we go through from here to there.

But right now you're probably in a stage that's pretty comfortable (or you'd be trying to get out of it). The comfort zone. The problem with a comfort zone is *the dream isn't in it.* It sure would be nice if it was. But it isn't.

So we have to be willing to take a step forward, out of comfort and toward the unknown territory. Just one step at a time.

—BRUCE WILKINSON, *The Dream Giver*

Lord, help me not to cling to what I know, but to cling to You.

WEEKEND

Your Shepherd Is the Lord

"I am the good shepherd. The good shepherd lays down his life for the sheep. The hired hand is not the shepherd who owns the sheep. So when he sees the wolf coming, he abandons the sheep and runs away. Then the wolf attacks the flock and scatters it."

John 10:11–12

The Lord is your Shepherd. Your Shepherd is the Lord. And it's important to know that the word *Lord* identifies God from the standpoint of His self-existence and self-sufficiency. In other words, God does not have to go outside of Himself to be God. That's good for us to know, because it means we don't have to go outside of God to get help from God. God is complete within Himself.

It's because so many Christians do not truly believe in the sufficiency of the Lord that they get small lords, better known as idols, to meet their needs. Trust that the Lord—capital *L*—is self-sufficient, eternal, totally complete within Himself. You can let Him be your Shepherd.

—Tony Evans, *God Is More than Enough*

Lord, help me to believe more fully that You are sufficient.

MONDAY

Putting on My True Clothes

Colossians 3:12–17

Therefore, as God's chosen people, holy and dearly loved, clothe yourselves with compassion, kindness, humility, gentleness and patience. Bear with each other and forgive whatever grievances you may have against one another. Forgive as the Lord forgave you. And over all these virtues put on love, which binds them all together in perfect unity. Let the peace of Christ rule in your hearts, since as members of one body you were called to peace. And be thankful. Let the word of Christ dwell in you richly as you teach and admonish one another with all wisdom, and as you sing psalms, hymns and spiritual songs with gratitude in your hearts to God. And whatever you do, whether in word or deed, do it all in the name of the Lord Jesus, giving thanks to God the Father through him.

Father, please don't let me start my day without clothing myself in keeping with who I am as Your child.

TUESDAY

As GM Goes...

"Do not store up for yourselves treasures on earth, where moth and rust destroy, and where thieves break in and steal. But store up for yourselves treasures in heaven, where moth and rust do not destroy, and where thieves do not break in and steal. For where your treasure is, there your heart will be also."

Matthew 6:19–21

Jesus makes clear in Matthew 6 that our hearts always go where we put our money, which of course is actually God's money.

If you want to get a heart for, say, General Motors or Microsoft, there's an easy way to do it. You buy up shares of the company.

That's really what we're doing when we're giving. We're buying ourselves shares in the kingdom of God. We're developing vested interest in God's kingdom.

Let's say there's an earthquake in India. If you have been investing in church planting and literature distribution, for instance, in that country you will be motivated to pray for and help the people affected by the quake.

Where your treasure is, there your heart will be also.

—Randy Alcorn, *The Treasure Principle*

Lord, help me to be aware of where I'm investing my heart.

WEDNESDAY

The Good News of Church

His intent was that now, through the church, the manifold wisdom of God should be made known to the rulers and authorities in the heavenly realms, according to his eternal purpose which he accomplished in Christ Jesus our Lord. In him and through faith in him we may approach God with freedom and confidence.

Ephesians 3:10–12

Hey, I've got some good news for you. If you're a Christian, you're familiar with this good news.

It's called the gospel. It's the message that God sent His only Son, Jesus Christ, to die for our sins in our place so that all who put their trust in Jesus can be forgiven. But why does that mean we need to be a part of a church, with people who annoy us?

Let me show you the connection. The church is the vehicle God has chosen to take the Good News of the gospel to every generation. The church demonstrates to the watching world the transformation that takes place because Jesus died for our sins.

Every person who's experienced the power of the Good News needs to have a love and a passion for the local church.

—Joshua Harris, *Stop Dating the Church*

Lord, help me to demonstrate the gospel through Your church.

THURSDAY

Born to Worship

The fear of the Lord is the beginning of knowledge.

Proverbs 1:7

You're going to spend your entire life worshiping. You don't have an option. You cannot be exempt. You can't check out. You can't sign a waiver and say, "No, I'm not going to spend my life worshiping. I don't want to do that. I don't even believe in God. I'm not even a part of this thing. I'm an atheist, for crying out loud. I'm not going to spend my life worshiping."

Oh yeah, you are. Everybody's got something on the throne. Everybody has something of highest value. Everybody's bending their life around the value of somebody or something. And the tragedy is that you could spend your entire life worshiping something less than worthy.

What's on the throne in the center of your life?

—Louie Giglio, *The Air I Breathe*

Lord, help me to put You first in my life
as Lord of everything I do, think, or know.

FRIDAY

Imparting Grace

Do not let any unwholesome talk come out of your mouths, but only what is helpful for building others up according to their needs, that it may benefit those who listen. And do not grieve the Holy Spirit of God, with whom you were sealed for the day of redemption.

Ephesians 4:29–30

Our words are very powerful. I call them *life words* and *death words*. I've known many grown men and women who still wince or even tear up when they recall death words their parents or teachers or some other significant adult uttered years before. ("Be careful!" "Sorry, Dad." "Way to go, Einstein." "What an idiot!")

The apostle Paul teaches that our words can harm, or they can build up and give life. Be careful to "impart grace to the hearer," rather than corruption.

—Richard Blackaby, *Putting a Face on Grace*

Lord, may my mouth speak grace to others.

WEEKEND

God's Best

Hebrews 1:1–4

In the past God spoke to our forefathers through the prophets at many times and in various ways, but in these last days he has spoken to us by his Son, whom he appointed heir of all things, and through whom he made the universe. The Son is the radiance of God's glory and the exact representation of his being, sustaining all things by his powerful word. After he had provided purification for sins, he sat down at the right hand of the Majesty in heaven. So he became as much superior to the angels as the name he has inherited is superior to theirs.

Lord, truly You have saved Your very best for me:
Your own perfect Son. May my heart worship Him alone today.

MONDAY

No Matter What

If we hope for what we do not yet have, we wait for it patiently.

Romans 8:25

An allegorical tale of a Nobody named Ordinary from the town of Familiar.

Ordinary had never dared to walk this way before, but like every Nobody, he knew that the farther you walked from the center of Familiar, the less familiar things became. He also knew that most Nobodies who tried to leave the comfort zone of Familiar became so uncomfortable, they turned around and went home. Some were so glad to be back, they sat in their recliner for days waiting for nothing to happen and sighed with relief.

But Ordinary told himself that he was different from most Nobodies. He would pursue his dream no matter what. Brimming with anticipation, Ordinary whistled his new tune while he walked, and he dreamed about the great things he would accomplish. Life had never been so promising.

—Bruce Wilkinson, *The Dream Giver*

Lord, help me to keep on the path You've set me on,
even if it starts to get scary.

TUESDAY

Running to God

So he said to me, "This is the word of the Lord *to Zerubbabel: 'Not by might nor by power, but by my Spirit,' says the* Lord *Almighty."*

Zechariah 4:6

Anybody here besides me exhaust themselves trying to play God in their life? It's exhausting, isn't it? And God says, *You-hoo. Up here. Got some answers for you. Rest in Me.*

So many times we run to everyone but our Lord. I'm sure it breaks God's heart. We will tell a perfect stranger who might be doing our hair or taking our money in a grocery store. They ask, "How're you doing?" and we'll give them an earful. But we will not go to our Lord, who truly cares.

You know what? The Word of God does not say, "Be anxious for everything and let all your requests be known to anyone who's willing to listen to you." It says, "I am the Lord all-powerful, so don't depend on your own strength, but on My Spirit."

We're not doing justice to anyone by not letting God have the glory in our circumstances. We need to set an example of what it looks like to run to God.

—Sheri Rose Shepherd, *My Prince Will Come*

Lord, help me to run to You and not rely on my own strength.

WEDNESDAY

When to Say No

Do not love the world or anything in the world. If anyone loves the world, the love of the Father is not in him. For everything in the world—the cravings of sinful man, the lust of his eyes and the boasting of what he has and does—comes not from the Father but from the world. The world and its desires pass away, but the man who does the will of God lives forever.

1 John 2:15–17

Most of us live our lives on the edge. We have bulging schedules and maxed-out credit cards, and we collapse at the end of the day in sheer exhaustion. What we need is margin.

What does that mean? It means we have to learn the power of the word *No,* so that we can say *Yes* to what really matters—whether it's in our finances, our relationships, or our activities and commitments.

Learn the power of saying no more often than yes. Build some needed margin into your life.

—Dennis and Barbara Rainey, *Pressure Proof Your Marriage*

Lord, help me to learn to say no.

THURSDAY

Tale of Two Trails

Surely you desire truth in the inner parts;
you teach me wisdom in the inmost place.
Cleanse me with hyssop, and I will be clean;
wash me, and I will be whiter than snow.
Let me hear joy and gladness;
let the bones you have crushed rejoice.

Psalm 51:6–8

I'd like you to visualize two trails. One is very neat and beautiful, well traveled. The other has deep, ugly ruts that go into the ditch. It looks awful.

Well, when two feet of snow comes, you can't tell the difference between the one trail or the other. Those trails represent lives. Here's a person who's lived a good life. Here's another person who has really blown it. But after God's forgiveness both lives appear the same to our Lord. "Come now, let us reason together," says the Lord, "though your sins are like scarlet, they shall be as white as snow."

—Erwin Lutzer, *After You've Blown It*

Lord, thank You for cleansing me and giving me gladness.

FRIDAY

Not of Yourselves

Praise be to the God and Father of our Lord Jesus Christ,
who has blessed us in the heavenly realms with every spiritual blessing in Christ.
For he chose us in him before the creation of the world to be holy and blameless
in his sight. In love he predestined us to be adopted as his sons through
Jesus Christ, in accordance with his pleasure and will—to the praise of his
glorious grace, which he has freely given us in the One he loves.

Ephesians 1:3–6

Superstition and legalism are two great realities in the Eastern world. Superstition comes from the fear that unless you do certain things, what follows can be very serious for you. Legalism carries that a step further. There are certain laws you need to live by to make sure that you meet the demands of the power that ultimately controls the universe—whatever you wish to call it.

Isn't it fascinating that Jesus Christ delivers us from both of them? He tells us that it is not by the keeping of the law that we come to Him. "For by grace are you saved through faith and that not of yourselves. It is the gift of God."

—Ravi Zacharias, *The Lotus and the Cross*

Lord, thank You for the gift of salvation.

WEEKEND

SUFFERING CONSEQUENCES

"You have heard that it was said, 'Do not commit adultery.' But I tell you that anyone who looks at a woman lustfully has already committed adultery with her in his heart."

MATTHEW 5:27–28

Movies and made-for-television shows about the story of David and Bathsheba usually paint their palace life as rich and lavish. Everything's first class. Everything's wonderful. They never show the consequences. They never show what devastation their adultery was to David's family and to his children, not to mention Bathsheba's husband, whose death David arranged.

The devil always says don't worry, there won't be any consequences. But God knows there will be. Maybe not tomorrow or the next day, but eventually. David and Bathsheba discovered that was true. That's why God forbids it.

—RON MEHL, *Right with God*

Lord, help me to realize that You give laws for our good, and when we break them there are serious consequences.

MONDAY

Impacting the World

He has showed you, O man, what is good.
And what does the Lord *require of you?*
To act justly and to love mercy
and to walk humbly with your God.

Micah 6:8

We as Christians need to be willing to stop and have a quick conversation with people we come across, even if it's just to say, "Hey, how are you doing today?" That can have a phenomenal impact.

There are of course broader ways we can impact the men and women around the world who are needy. Maybe God is calling you to go and have a more tangible impact, a longer-term impact in different places. Be willing to step out. How is God going to use you, and how does He want you to step out of your comfort zone to have an impact in this world for His kingdom?

Seek Him first. What is it He wants you to do?

—Mike Yankoski, *Under the Overpass*

Lord, help me to act justly, love mercy, and
walk humbly with You.

TUESDAY

Believing and Belonging

All the believers were together and had everything in common.
Selling their possessions and goods, they gave to anyone as he had need.
Every day they continued to meet together in the temple courts.
They broke bread in their homes and ate together with glad and sincere hearts,
praising God and enjoying the favor of all the people.

Acts 2:44-47

Experts today describe Christians in America as being believers, but not belongers. In other words, we will express faith in Jesus Christ, we'll maybe read our Bibles, but we're not really interested in being a part of a community of faith, of giving ourselves to involvement in the local church.

I think Scripture is very clear that we're called to not only be believers, but we're also called to be belongers. We need to give ourselves to the local church, the body of Christ. It's in the local church that these transformed individuals come together into a new family, and together our changed lives bear witness to the reality of Jesus Christ.

—Joshua Harris, *Stop Dating the Church*

Lord, help me to seek ways to participate more fully in Your church.

WEDNESDAY

Into the Wasteland

I cry aloud to the LORD; I lift up my voice to the LORD for mercy.
I pour out my complaint before him; before him I tell my trouble.
When my spirit grows faint within me, it is you who know my way.

PSALM 142:1–3

God often puts me in contact with leaders who seem to be stuck in a wasteland. And they misinterpret it, just as I used to misinterpret it. That is, that it's a waste.

In the wasteland it feels as if no matter what you do, you cannot move forward. No matter how hard you pray, you don't get a yes. And in time, you can become really angry at God and feel as if He has betrayed you. That's because it's hard to understand the purpose of something that seems such a waste.

But it's not. God wants you to break through the borderland—the comfort zone. He will bring you into the wasteland for one reason and one reason alone: to prepare you to do the dream.

—BRUCE WILKINSON, *The Dream Giver*

Lord, thank You that in Your plan for my life nothing is wasted.

THURSDAY

God Reigns

Psalm 47

Clap your hands, all you nations;
shout to God with cries of joy.
How awesome is the Lord *Most High,*
the great King over all the earth!
He subdued nations under us,
peoples under our feet.
He chose our inheritance for us,
the pride of Jacob, whom he loved. Selah
God has ascended amid shouts of joy,
the Lord *amid the sounding of trumpets.*
Sing praises to God, sing praises;
sing praises to our King, sing praises.
For God is the King of all the earth;
sing to him a psalm of praise.
God reigns over the nations;
God is seated on his holy throne.
The nobles of the nations assemble
as the people of the God of Abraham,
for the kings of the earth belong to God;
he is greatly exalted.

Lord, how great You are!

FRIDAY

Graceless Christians

Be wise in the way you act toward outsiders;
make the most of every opportunity. Let your conversation be always
full of grace, seasoned with salt, so that you may know how to answer everyone.

Colossians 4:5–7

I think one of the great paradoxes of the Christian life is what I call the Paradox of Graceless Christians.

To become a Christian you had to have experienced the grace of God, which of course is undeserved forgiveness and favor. Yet the amazing thing is how many people who have been saved by grace are unwilling to show grace to other people. These are Christians who are intolerant of people's shortcomings, critical of people's failures, cynical about people's possibilities of improvement and making changes, and unwilling to forgive someone who has offended them.

Don't be a person who has enjoyed God's grace in you own life but is unwilling to show it to others.

—Richard Blackaby, *Putting a Face on Grace*

Lord, help me not to be a graceless Christian,
but to show forgiveness and favor to all those around me.

WEEKEND

Cultural Affinity

Here there is no Greek or Jew, circumcised or uncircumcised, barbarian, Scythian, slave or free, but Christ is all, and is in all.

Colossians 3:11

One of the big catchwords today is *community*. We all want it. We all want relationship. We all want to be able to let our guard down. But when you look across the landscape of American culture, you find what we really want—instead of biblical community, cultural affinity. I want to go to a church where everyone is like me. They listen to the kind of music I like. They wear the same kind of clothes I like.

The great thing about Jesus is that when He came to the earth and He banded us together and said, "You will be one in me," it meant that no matter who is in the room, if they're a Christ follower, you are one with them. And it's not your music that causes you to have something in common or your socio-economic status or the type of clothes you wear, but it's Jesus.

—Rick McKinley, *Jesus in the Margins*

Lord, help me to love my brothers and sisters in Christ, regardless of what they look like.

MONDAY

His Bride

Let us rejoice and be glad and give him glory! For the wedding of the Lamb has come, and his bride has made herself ready.

Revelation 19:7

The Bible uses a lot of metaphors to describe the church. We're called a building. We're called a body. But there's one metaphor in particular that I really find amazing. That is where Jesus described the church as His bride.

I remember when I was being married, and my wife, Shannon, was walking down the aisle. I got a glimpse of the passion and love and patience Jesus has for us. Every time I think about it I am reminded that I can never give up on the church. I can never come up with all the reasons that it's letting me down, because Jesus has never given up on the church. After all these years, after all of the mistakes that we've made, He still calls us His bride.

—Joshua Harris, *Stop Dating the Church*

Lord, help me to see how precious
You view Your bride, the church.

TUESDAY

Standard in Giving

Now he who supplies seed to the sower and bread for food will also supply and increase your store of seed and will enlarge the harvest of your righteousness. You will be made rich in every way so that you can be generous on every occasion, and through us your generosity will result in thanksgiving to God.

2 Corinthians 9:10–11

How do you fill in the blank here? "You will be made rich in every way so that—"

How we finish the sentence after the *so that* is critically important. One school of thought, known as prosperity theology, would finish it "—so that we might live in wealth and show the world how much God blesses those who love Him." But that is not how the apostle Paul completes his thought. He says, "You will be made rich in every way *so that you can be generous on every occasion.*"

The principle is this: God prospers us, not to raise our standard living, but to raise our standard of giving.

—Randy Alcorn, *The Treasure Principle*

Lord, help me to be aware of how generous I am, or am not, with the wealth You give me.

WEDNESDAY

Known by More than Reputation

"I am the good shepherd; I know my sheep and my sheep know me—
just as the Father knows me and I know the Father—
and I lay down my life for the sheep."

John 10:14–15

Do you know God by name? Does the Word of God come off the pages and become part of your life? Or are you so distant from God that you know Him only by reputation?

God's passion for each one of us is an intimate relationship. He does not want religious institutionalism. He wants to relate to us as a shepherd relates to his sheep, on an intimate, personal level. Why? What God wants is closeness, and only when there's closeness do you experience God.

Seek Him face-to-face. Let Him be involved in your life.

—Tony Evans, *God Is More than Enough*

Lord, help me to seek You daily
for a closer relationship.

THURSDAY

The Right Choice

Consider him who endured such opposition from sinful men, so that you will not grow weary and lose heart. In your struggle against sin, you have not yet resisted to the point of shedding your blood.

Hebrews 12:3–4

Has this ever happened to you? Your boss says, "If Mrs. Williams calls, tell her I'm out of the office, okay?"

We all like to be comfortable and popular. But what happens if the right choice isn't comfortable or popular? Do we choose what's right, or do we do what's easy?

Making the kingdom a priority means being committed to goodness, righteousness, and truth. Sometimes it causes conflict. Sometimes it makes us unpopular. Sometimes it can be threatening to our very well-being. When we as Christians make the kingdom of God our first priority, it's not always easy. But it is always right.

—Stuart Briscoe, *Time Bandits*

Lord, help me to stay firm on the basics of the kingdom.

FRIDAY

No Backtracking

All the Israelites grumbled against Moses and Aaron, and the whole assembly said to them, "If only we had died in Egypt! Or in this desert! Why is the Lord bringing us to this land only to let us fall by the sword? Our wives and children will be taken as plunder. Wouldn't it be better for us to go back to Egypt?"

Numbers 14:2–3

An allegorical tale of a Nobody named Ordinary from the town of Familiar.

With every step back toward the middle of Familiar, Ordinary grew more comfortable. But he quickly noticed he was also growing sad again. He knew why. With each step he took, he was leaving his big dream farther behind. Then he heard the Dream Giver again.

"Why are you going back?" he asked. Ordinary stopped.

"Because I'm afraid. Leaving Familiar feels too scary and too risky," he said.

"Yes it does."

"But if I was supposed to do this big dream," he explained, "then I'm sure I wouldn't feel so afraid."

"Yes, you would," said the Dream Giver. "Every Nobody does."

—Bruce Wilkinson, *The Dream Giver*

Lord, help me to persevere despite fear.

WEEKEND

Glorious Intruder

Good and upright is the Lord; therefore he instructs sinners in his ways.
He guides the humble in what is right and teaches them his way.
All the ways of the Lord are loving and faithful for those
who keep the demands of his covenant.

Psalm 25:8–10

God is an intruder.

He crashes the party, throws open locked doors, hits the light switch in a dark room. God is a glorious intruder in your life, your thoughts, your pain. The Spirit of the Lord even invades you, taking up residence in your very body. What can we do but marvel in speechless wonder at our powerful and almighty God, who, incidentally, has every right to intrude?

Day by day, moment by moment, God monitors your thoughts, your concerns, your anxieties, and the deep-down fears that no one else knows but you. Invite Him into your thoughts, your plans, your concerns, and He says, "I will come in."

—Joni Eareckson Tada, *31 Days to Intimacy with God*

Lord, help me to open my entire life to you
and listen to Your guidance.

MONDAY

How to Grow

Therefore confess your sins to each other and pray for each other so that you may be healed. The prayer of a righteous man is powerful and effective.... My brothers, if one of you should wander from the truth and someone should bring him back, remember this: Whoever turns a sinner from the error of his way will save him from death and cover over a multitude of sins.

James 5:16, 19–20

You don't have to go to church to get saved. You can say a prayer to God. You can put your trust in Jesus Christ and be saved right where you are and never set foot in a church. But it's clear throughout Scripture that if you genuinely turn from your sins and experience the new life that's made available through Jesus Christ, you're going to join yourself with a local body of believers.

The reason why is that God uses pastors and other Christians in our lives to help us grow. So one of the important parts of demonstrating that you've experienced the new life is to live that new life out in the new community of the local church.

—Joshua Harris, *Stop Dating the Church*

Lord, help me to seek out new believers and help them grow.

TUESDAY

User-Friendly Version

Crave pure spiritual milk, so that by it you may grow up in your salvation.

1 Peter 2:2

"What's that?"

"It's my new UFV Bible."

"UFV?"

"User-Friendly Version."

"It's like one piece of paper, man."

"Yeah, it's kind of a paraphrase."

The three-point sermon is popular right now. You know, three points on how the Bible can better organize your life. Or three points that are going to make your life happier and easier.

But Christ designed a unique, special life for me that's different from what He designed for you. It's not pray this, do that, and you'll have this. It's an ongoing, daily process of following Him, of really being a true follower of God. That will give you the abundant life. There's no three-step process. It's a lifelong process of following God.

—Ryan Dobson, *2 Live 4*

Lord, help me to seek to grow in You.

WEDNESDAY

Our Prince Will Come

Then I saw a new heaven and a new earth, for the first heaven and the first earth had passed away, and there was no longer any sea. I saw the Holy City, the new Jerusalem, coming down out of heaven from God, prepared as a bride beautifully dressed for her husband. And I heard a loud voice from the throne saying, "Now the dwelling of God is with men, and he will live with them. They will be his people, and God himself will be with them and be their God."

REVELATIONS 21:1–3

Someday our Prince will come.

The Word of God describes the new Jerusalem like a bride dressed in her wedding gown, ready to meet her husband. When you're young, you think you're going to live happily ever after. The truth is, we *are* going to live happily ever after.

Our King—the Prince who's coming to get us—says, "No eyes have seen, no ears have heard all that I have prepared for those who love me."

—SHERI ROSE SHEPHERD, *My Prince Will Come*

Lord, thank You for the hope of heaven.

THURSDAY

Born of God

1 John 5:1–5

Everyone who believes that Jesus is the Christ is born of God, and everyone who loves the father loves his child as well. This is how we know that we love the children of God: by loving God and carrying out his commands. This is love for God: to obey his commands. And his commands are not burdensome, for everyone born of God overcomes the world. This is the victory that has overcome the world, even our faith. Who is it that overcomes the world? Only he who believes that Jesus is the Son of God.

Lord, may I not confuse the feeling of love for acts of love. May I prove that I am Your child by my obedience today.

FRIDAY

What Is Important

"If you love those who love you, what credit is that to you? Even 'sinners' love those who love them. And if you do good to those who are good to you, what credit is that to you? Even 'sinners' do that.... But love your enemies, do good to them, and lend to them without expecting to get anything back. Then your reward will be great, and you will be sons of the Most High, because he is kind to the ungrateful and wicked."

Luke 6:32–33, 35–36

Grace recognizes what's important and what isn't. Unfortunately some people get things confused. They emphasize things that don't really matter. Like performance. Some parents express disappointment if their children do not get all A's on their report card or don't make first string on the team or didn't win an award or a scholarship. Inadvertently what they are doing is saying that things or reputations or achievements are more important that people themselves.

Grace always recognizes that people are what is important. Relationships are what is important. And grace focuses on those things.

—Richard Blackaby, *Putting a Face on Grace*

Lord, help me to always put people first.

WEEKEND

Come to Jesus

Record my lament; list my tears on your scroll—
are they not in your record?

Psalm 56:8

Your heart is breaking and you're hurting. What if you were to invite Jesus to visit with you over a cup of coffee or tea? What would He say? I think He might share something along this line.

I've got some good news for you. I'm right here. I'm with you. I want to comfort you, and I'm going to heal your broken heart. Right now. At this very moment, I'm pushing back hell and I'm fighting battles for you. Before long, you're going to experience the spoils of victory. Come to Me. Keep coming to Me. Allow My Spirit to touch your wounds, and I promise you—I promise you—I will replace that devastation and I will replace that despair with My spirit of gladness and joy. This isn't something you're going to be able to do on your own. Keep coming to Me. I'm here for you.

—Dr. Steve Stephens & Pam Vredevelt, *The Wounded Woman*

Lord, thank You for seeking me out
when I am hurting.

MONDAY

Idol Dreams

When Christ, who is your life, appears, then you also will appear with him in glory. Put to death, therefore, whatever belongs to your earthly nature: sexual immorality, impurity, lust, evil desires and greed, which is idolatry.

Colossians 3:4–5

An allegorical tale of a character named Ordinary from the town of Familiar.

The Summit is the highest place in Dream Land. It is the place where the first time you're able to see the dream in all of its glory. And then you hear something that you can't believe.

You hear the Dream Giver ask you this question: "Give Me the dream. Give Me your dream." And everything in your heart says, "No, I can't give you the dream. I have sacrificed all this to get here? More parts of my personal dream died along the route. I'm finally in reach of this. What do you mean, 'Give Me the dream'?"

Without us knowing it, the dream has become more important to us than the Dream Giver. And it's become an idol.

—Bruce Wilkinson, *The Dream Giver*

Lord, help me not to let my dream become more important than You.

TUESDAY

The American Dream Syndrome

I urge, then, first of all, that requests, prayers, intercession and thanksgiving be made for everyone...that we may live peaceful and quiet lives in all godliness and holiness. This is good, and pleases God our Savior.

1 Timothy 2:1–3

Whether you know it or not, your relationships are susceptible to the American Dream Syndrome.

We are sold the notion that we can have it all. And that we deserve to have it all. The unwritten motto of the American Dream Syndrome is *The more stuff you have, the better off you'll be.*

Do you know what? With that philosophy, all you'll do is compare yourself with the Joneses. The Scriptures point out that at life's end, our stash will be empty and we will stand before God alone. No fancy houses. No shiny cars. No handsome or beautiful spouse. Listen to the apostle Paul when he teaches us that godliness is actually a means of great gain, when accompanied with contentment.

—Dennis and Barbara Rainey, *Pressure Proof Your Marriage*

Lord, help me to relinquish my possessions, which You own anyway.

WEDNESDAY

Shout for Joy

Psalm 100

Shout for joy to the Lord, all the earth.
Worship the Lord with gladness;
come before him with joyful songs.
Know that the Lord is God.
It is he who made us, and we are his;
we are his people, the sheep of his pasture.
Enter his gates with thanksgiving
and his courts with praise;
give thanks to him and praise his name.
For the Lord is good and his love endures forever;
his faithfulness continues through all generations.

Lord, thank You that You have made us Your people.

THURSDAY

With No Thought of Yourself

"If that is how God clothes the grass of the field, which is here today and tomorrow is thrown into the fire, will he not much more clothe you, O you of little faith? So do not worry, saying, 'What shall we eat?' or 'What shall we drink?' or 'What shall we wear?'"

Matthew 6:30–31

What would you do for God if you weren't concerned with what you wore, what you ate, where you slept, what you owned, what people thought of you, or what discomforts you might face?

By stepping out in faith, away from your comfort zone, into the full grace of the Lord Jesus Christ, He will meet all your needs. Yes, it may be difficult, but in doing so, He can use you to change this world in tangible ways with every single person that you come across. By not caring what you're going to eat, where you're going to sleep, what you're going to do, you open yourself up to be used to change this world for our Lord and Savior, Jesus Christ.

—Mike Yankoski, *Under the Overpass*

Lord, help me to act as if my outward appearance does not matter.

FRIDAY

The Surprises of Prayer

"Because they lead my people astray, saying, 'Peace,' when there is no peace, and because, when a flimsy wall is built, they cover it with whitewash, therefore tell those who cover it with whitewash that it is going to fall.... When the wall collapses, will people not ask you, 'Where is the whitewash you covered it with?'"

EZEKIEL 13:10–12

Prayer couches two surprises.

First, God listens when we pray. Jesus, Himself, assures us of that. "Ask, and it will be given to you," He said. If you believe, you will receive whatever you ask for in prayer. You may not turn the head of your teacher or keep the attention of your spouse, but when you pray, God pauses.

The second surprise is, we seldom pray. We have the greatest privilege imaginable, access to the very control center of the universe, yet we rarely use it. Our lack of prayer surprises even God. Through the prophet Ezekiel, He lamented, "I looked for a man among them who would build up the wall and stand before me in the gap on behalf of the land so I would not have to destroy it, but I found none" (Ezekiel 22:30).

—MAX LUCADO, *Turn*

Lord, help me to pray regularly and expectantly.

WEEKEND

Seeking a Church

Speaking the truth in love, we will in all things grow up into him who is the Head, that is, Christ. From him the whole body, joined and held together by every supporting ligament, grows and builds itself up in love, as each part does its work.

Ephesians 4:15–16

I'm challenging people to stop dating the church, to leave behind a consumer mentality and stop the church-hopping; to settle down in one place and give their lives away in a local church.

Yet there are times in which people need to "shop" for a church. Perhaps they are a new Christian, or they've moved to a new area, or they've realized that the gathering they're in isn't right for them. In these kinds of situations, it's important to ask the right questions about a local church. Questions such as, are the believers being guided by God's Word? Are they teaching and living by God's Word?

There will be differences in style of worship and so on anywhere you go. We want to make sure the qualities that God says are important are guiding us.

—Joshua Harris, *Stop Dating the Church*

Lord, help me to replace my consumer mentality with commitment.

MONDAY

Here I Am

In you, O Lord, I have taken refuge; let me never be put to shame.

Psalm 71:1

I was at a camp. I was a kid and I just loved being at this camp and I loved being with friends. And we were singing out these songs to God, just singing our hearts out to God. And all of a sudden I sensed God speaking to me.

I'd never had this before. I never even knew what this was, but I sensed inside of me that God was calling me. I ran out of the back of the service. I couldn't handle it. I couldn't be in there anymore. I didn't need to hear any speakers because God was speaking to me.

I found this tree and knelt under it. I didn't even know what to say to God, but I knew He was saying something to me. I just said, "God, I don't even know what to say to You, but I'm just telling You, Lord, You have all of me for whatever You want for the rest of my days. Take all of me. Here I am."

—Chris Tomlin, *The Way I Was Made*

Lord, I am Yours.

TUESDAY

Heavenly Meeting

Praise be to the God and Father of our Lord Jesus Christ! In his great mercy he has given us new birth into a living hope through the resurrection of Jesus Christ from the dead, and into an inheritance that can never perish, spoil or fade—kept in heaven for you.

1 Peter 1:3–4

One of the great things about giving is being able to look forward to being greeted in heaven by people whose lives have been touched and changed through our giving.

We're going to have the opportunity to thank people for what they invested in our lives. And we're also going to have the wonderful experience of having people thank us that we were faithful in our giving.

Some of those will be people we know here on earth. Some of them will be people we've never met, until we meet them in heaven, and to put our arms around each other and say, "Thank you. Thank you for giving to the Lord." What a wonderful thing that's going to be.

—Randy Alcorn, *The Treasure Principle*

Lord, help me to live today as if preparing for that meeting in heaven.

WEDNESDAY

His Hand of Power

"I baptize you with water for repentance. But after me will come one who is more powerful than I, whose sandals I am not fit to carry. He will baptize you with the Holy Spirit and with fire."

Matthew 3:11

One of the most exciting things about reading the Bible is to come across those stories when God's power was revealed before the eyes of men. It's just so exhilarating to watch God intervene in time and space and do a miracle.

When you pray, "Dear God, would You please put Your hand upon me?" you're asking for God to open His hand of power for you. Has He done that recently? Have you been in a predicament where you needed His power because He has expanded your territory?

You know, it could be that you have not seen God's power recently because you have not asked for it. So ask Him. "God, would You please put Your hand of power upon me?"

—Bruce Wilkinson, *The Prayer of Jabez*

Lord, I need more of Your power in my life.

THURSDAY

The Rod and the Staff

Even though I walk
through the valley of the shadow of death,
I will fear no evil,
for you are with me;
your rod and your staff,
they comfort me.

Psalm 23:4

As our Shepherd, God has both a rod and a staff. The rod was used to ward off animals that would bring harm to the sheep. The staff would be used to reach and pull in a wayward sheep out of the thicket.

The rod is the protection of God. The staff is the grace of God. So God, like a good parent or shepherd, uses His rod to protect us, externally and internally. He uses His staff, grace, to reach us when we have wandered and steered away from Him. Why? Because He loves us.

—Tony Evans, *God Is More than Enough*

Lord, thank You that You care enough
to use Your rod and staff.

FRIDAY

"What Are You Making?"

Isaiah 45:9–12, 22

"Woe to him who quarrels with his Maker,
to him who is but a potsherd among the potsherds on the ground.
Does the clay say to the potter, 'What are you making?'
Does your work say, 'He has no hands'?
Woe to him who says to his father, 'What have you begotten?'
or to his mother, 'What have you brought to birth?"
This is what the Lord says—
the Holy One of Israel, and its Maker:
Concerning things to come,
do you question me about my children,
or give me orders about the work of my hands?
It is I who made the earth
and created mankind upon it.
My own hands stretched out the heavens;
I marshaled their starry hosts.
Turn to me and be saved, all you ends of the earth;
for I am God, and there is no other."

Lord, thank You for being the potter in my life.

WEEKEND

Trusting God with Our Worries

Do not be anxious about anything, but in everything, by prayer and petition, with thanksgiving, present your requests to God. And the peace of God, which transcends all understanding, will guard your hearts and your minds in Christ Jesus.

Philippians 4:6–7

Worry. It can ruin a perfectly good day. Maybe things were going great for you today, until you got that call from your son's principal or had that talk with your doctor. The stuff we worry about is important. If it wasn't, we wouldn't be worried. But are we making it too important?

Jesus tells us that the kingdom is more important than anything else. The fact is, when we worry, we aren't joyful. When we're anxious, we don't feel peace. But when we really trust God with everything and make His kingdom a priority, we'll experience a peace that surpasses our understanding and a joy that no report of bad news can steal.

—Stuart Briscoe, *Time Bandits*

Lord, help me to trust You, and fill me with peace.

MONDAY

Spiritual To-Do Lists

Be imitators of God, therefore, as dearly loved children and live a life of love, just as Christ loved us and gave himself up for us as a fragrant offering and sacrifice to God.

Ephesians 5:1–2

Sometimes I can feel like I have a spiritual to-do list that is two miles long. Do you know what I'm talking about?

I'm supposed to be reading my Bible. I need to be praying. I need to be a good husband, a good father. I need to make sure that I'm witnessing and on and on.

And what about the church? Is it just another to-do item that we have to add to our list? I view it differently because I believe that the local church is like a spiritual greenhouse. It's an environment that God has created. So you see, loving the church is not just another thing you need to do, it's the thing that God has called every Christian to do so that we can thrive and grow the way He wants us to.

—Joshua Harris, *Stop Dating the Church*

Lord, help me not to just check off actions I must take, but to imitate You and love Your children.

TUESDAY

The God of Heaven

Daniel 2:19–23

Then Daniel praised the God of heaven and said:
"Praise be to the name of God for ever and ever;
wisdom and power are his.
He changes times and seasons;
he sets up kings and deposes them.
He gives wisdom to the wise
and knowledge to the discerning.
He reveals deep and hidden things;
he knows what lies in darkness,
and light dwells with him.
I thank and praise you, O God of my fathers:
You have given me wisdom and power,
you have made known to me what we asked of you,
you have made known to us the dream of the king."

Lord, thank You that You are wise and powerful.

WEDNESDAY

God's Grammar Lesson

"You did not choose me, but I chose you and appointed you
to go and bear fruit—fruit that will last.
Then the Father will give you whatever you ask in my name."

John 15:16

I know we all have reasons to not feel like a princess or prince. I've been a part of five blended families. My parents have been married and divorced three times each. My father was a Hollywood disk jockey and my mother was an actress and a model, and she had her own TV show. When I was in high school, I had an English teacher walk up to me and say in front of everybody, "Sheri Rose, you were born to lose in life. You will never amount to anything."

Praise the Lord that she did not teach God's grammar lesson. Do you know what God's grammar lesson is? *Don't put a period where I have a comma, because I have a plan for every life I create.*

—Sheri Rose Shepherd, *My Prince Will Come*

Lord, thank You that You had a plan for my life.

THURSDAY

Sabbath Rest

For in six days the Lord made the heavens and the earth, the sea,
and all that is in them, but he rested on the seventh day.
Therefore the Lord blessed the Sabbath day and made it holy.

Exodus 20:11

One of the reasons we are so hurried and hectic today in our pace of life is because we have lost the art of practicing Sabbath rest.

Taking a day and honoring God by resting from our harried lifestyles is not only healthful; it's spiritually beneficial. God commands us to observe the Sabbath. It is His invitation for us to draw near to Him. That's how He helps to detoxify us from the pressures of the culture we live in. Keep the Sabbath.

—Dennis and Barbara Rainey, *Pressure Proof Your Marriage*

Lord, help me to make Sabbath rest a priority.

FRIDAY

Thinking to Ask

"Ask and it will be given to you; seek and you will find; knock and the door will be opened to you. For everyone who asks receives; he who seeks finds; and to him who knocks, the door will be opened."

MATTHEW 7:7–8

It was ten o'clock at night and my daughter came up to me and said, "Dad, I would love to have some pepperoni pizza. Can you order some?" I looked at her and smiled and said, "Sweetheart, that sounds great."

Well, while we were eating that same pizza, she looked at me with kind of an interesting look and said, "Dad, would you have ordered the pizza if I hadn't asked for it?" I said, "It never even entered my mind. I wasn't thinking about pizza until you asked."

Remember Jesus said, "Ask and it shall be given to you." But do you know that Jesus didn't invite you to do that. Jesus commanded you. It's an imperative. He said, "I command you to ask." So my friend, what are you asking for today?

—BRUCE WILKINSON, *The Prayer of Jabez*

Lord, help me to obey Your wonderful command to ask of You.

WEEKEND

Saints and Sinners

When they had finished eating, Jesus said to Simon Peter, "Simon son of John, do you truly love me more than these?" "Yes, Lord," he said, "you know that I love you." Jesus said, "Feed my lambs."

John 21:15

It's very encouraging to realize that God can mightily use people who've blown it in their Christian walk.

Think, for example, of David, who committed two great sins. Peter, who denied the Lord Jesus Christ. And Moses, who spent time in the desert because of manslaughter. God used these people despite their failures. It has been said that every saint has a past and every sinner has a future.

My friend, I want you to know that the very fact that you are alive is proof that God still has something good for you to do.

—Erwin Lutzer, *After You've Blown It*

Lord, thank You for the opportunity to serve You despite my past.

MONDAY

Undeserved Honor

"Don't be afraid," David said to him, "for I will surely show you kindness for the sake of your father Jonathan. I will restore to you all the land that belonged to your grandfather Saul, and you will always eat at my table." Mephibosheth bowed down and said, "What is your servant, that you should notice a dead dog like me?"

2 Samuel 9:7–8

When David ascended to the throne, he wanted to honor the memory of his dear friend, Prince Jonathan, who had been killed in battle. David learned that Jonathan's son, Mephibosheth was alive, so King David sent for him. Mephibosheth, before his father's death an heir to the throne, arrived in great fear. But the king said, "Don't be afraid. I've asked you to come so I could be kind to you because of your father, Jonathan. You shall live here at my palace." Mephibosheth had thought that he might be killed, but the king wanted to dine with him. What had he done to deserve this honor? Absolutely nothing.

If today you feel unworthy to come into the King's presence, come anyway. No matter what your weakness or handicap or disability, the King says, "Come, and dine."

—Joni Eareckson Tada, *31 Days to Intimacy with God*

Lord, thank You for your invitation to dine.

TUESDAY

Behind the Mask

Search me, O God, and know my heart.
Test me and know my thoughts.
Point out anything in me that offends you
and lead me along the path of everlasting life.

Psalm 139:23–24

Emotional pain is a warning from the Lord. We need to pay attention to it. God is saying, "You have something I want."

If the gas light comes on in your car and you put a piece of tape over it, you're still going to run out of gas, aren't you? Many times that's what we do. We mask our emotions, and we feel guilty that we feel pain. We think we must not be godly because we're experiencing pain or depression or problems in our life.

But the Lord allows pain in our life—as He has in the lives of every man and woman in the Bible—for divine purposes: to get closer to Him.

—Sheri Rose Shepherd, *My Prince Will Come*

Lord, help me to recognize when You are pointing out areas of my life I'm hiding behind that need attention.

WEDNESDAY

Not Ashamed

Romans 1:16–17

I am not ashamed of the gospel,
because it is the power of God
for the salvation of everyone who believes:
first for the Jew, then for the Gentile.
For in the gospel a righteousness from God is revealed,
a righteousness that is by faith from first to last,
just as it is written: "The righteous will live by faith."

Lord, thank You for revealing Your righteousness
in the gospel and granting that righteousness to me by faith.
May I not be ashamed to tell others this news today.

THURSDAY

Putting Things in the Right Order

"Therefore, whoever humbles himself like this child is the greatest in the kingdom of heaven."

Matthew 18:4

There are two parts to solving a combination lock. First are the numbers, of course. But there's also the order in which you need to dial the numbers. When you get the numbers in the right order, the lock releases.

It's sort of like that with the kingdom of God. Jesus never condemned anyone for being interested in food, clothing, or the future. He was concerned about that stuff too. What He wanted His followers to know is that when we get everything out of order in relation to the kingdom of God, it can lead to worry and frustration. And when the kingdom is in the right place, everything else will be there too.

It's the combination that can unlock peace, joy, and a fulfilling life for all of us, because it honors the King and promotes the kingdom.

—Stuart Briscoe, *Time Bandits*

Lord, help me to keep the right balance in life.

FRIDAY

All for Us

Isaiah 53:3–8

He was despised and rejected by men,
a man of sorrows, and familiar with suffering.
Like one from whom men hide their faces
he was despised, and we esteemed him not.
Surely he took up our infirmities
and carried our sorrows,
yet we considered him stricken by God,
smitten by him, and afflicted.
But he was pierced for our transgressions,
he was crushed for our iniquities;
the punishment that brought us peace was upon him,
and by his wounds we are healed.
We all, like sheep, have gone astray,
each of us has turned to his own way;
and the Lord has laid on him
the iniquity of us all.

Lord, when I consider all that You have done for me in sending Jesus, I am overwhelmed. Thank You. May I live in gratefulness and faith.

WEEKEND

The Book

Nehemiah 8:8–10

They read from the Book of the Law of God, making it clear and giving the meaning so that the people could understand what was being read. Then Nehemiah the governor, Ezra the priest and scribe, and the Levites who were instructing the people said to them all, "This day is sacred to the Lord *your God. Do not mourn or weep." For all the people had been weeping as they listened to the words of the Law. Nehemiah said, "Go and enjoy choice food and sweet drinks, and send some to those who have nothing prepared. This day is sacred to our Lord. Do not grieve, for the joy of the Lord is your strength."*